THE MODERN ORACLE

HOW TO TAP INTO YOUR UNIQUE PSYCHIC POWERS

Katy-K

International Award Winning Psychic

First published by Ultimate World Publishing 2021
Copyright © 2021 Katy-K

ISBN

Paperback: 978-1-922497-52-9
Ebook: 978-1-922497-53-6

Katy-K has asserted her rights under the Copyright, Designs and Patents Act 1988 to be identified as the author of this work. The information in this book is based on the author's experiences and opinions. The publisher specifically disclaims responsibility for any adverse consequences which may result from use of the information contained herein. Permission to use information has been sought by the author. Any breaches will be rectified in further editions of the book.

All rights reserved. No part of this publication may be reproduced, stored in or introduced into a retrieval system, or transmitted in any form, or by any means (electronic, mechanical, photocopying, recording or otherwise) without the prior written permission of the author. Any person who does any unauthorised act in relation to this publication may be liable to criminal prosecution and civil claims for damages. Enquiries should be made through the publisher.

Cover design: Ultimate World Publishing
Layout and typesetting: Ultimate World Publishing
Editor: Anita Saunders
Book cover photo: Zakharchuk-Shutterstock.com

Ultimate World Publishing
Diamond Creek,
Victoria Australia 3089
www.writeabook.com.au

Testimonials

What people are saying about the book

An enchanting and inspiring novel that accompanies you on your spiritual journey.

A captivating and inspiring story. Katy-K's enchanting and warm nature reflects throughout her spiritual journey and educates the modern-day psychic.

Katy-K's warmth and uplifting energy shines throughout this beautiful memoir.

Tiarne Todd, musician and publicist

I enjoyed your book so much, it was an absolute pleasure to read! It would have to be one of the best I've read on this subject; there seemed to be so much information that you wrote so clearly and concisely.

So exciting that you were on the cover of the *Psychics Directory*, I was such a fan of that magazine and *Spheres: the Spirit Guide* back in the day!

Anita Saunders, editor

Visit *www.katy-k.com* for more testimonials.

Dedication

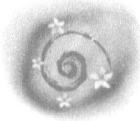

I dedicate this book to my family and friends and all the people who have assisted me on my journey. You all know who you are!

With love and deep gratitude for your encouragement and support to finally complete this long-awaited book.

Blessings to you all
Katy-K

Contents

Testimonials	iii
Dedication	v
Preface	1
Introduction: Welcome to the 'Modern Oracle'	7
The Shutdown	11
Keeping a Psychic Journal	19
I Want to Be More Psychic!	23
Off to Hogwarts	27
Psychics in the Family Tree	35
How Do I Know If I Am Psychic?	39
Trust and Belief	47
You Are Unique!	59
Validation of Meditation	65
Psychic Protection	77
Intention	87

Proof of Connection: Cooking With Yaya	95
Messages From Beyond: Proof of Life After Death	105
Readings	113
Psychic Tools	121
Signs and Synchronicity: Show Me a Sign	131
Animal Communication: If I Could Talk to the Animals	137
Ley Lines and Sacred Sites	145
Life as a Psychic	153
Testimonials	159
Offers	171
Contact Details for Katy-K	173
About the Author	175
Speakers Bio	177

Preface

When the student is ready the teacher will appear. When the student is truly ready ... The teacher will disappear

—Lao Tzu.

Have you ever had that unsettled feeling that something is just not right, but you don't know what it is? A persistent feeling that just won't go away and sometimes gets worse with time, leaving you puzzled and sometimes fearful.

Are you that person that has weird stuff happen to or around you? By weird, I mean some kind of metaphysical 'woo-woo' (unconventional beliefs regarded as having little or no scientific basis, especially those relating to spirituality, mysticism, or alternative medicine—*Oxford Languages*). You know, unexplained events: lights flickering on and off when you enter a room; electronics doing their own thing and not responding in the way that they should; curtains moving when there is no breeze or reason to move; the radio or windscreen wipers in your car turning on unassisted; or do you think of someone you haven't seen for some time and then they contact you? I could go on to list so much more. So, do you ever wonder why weird things are happening to you? Are you curious to explore more about yourself and your intuitive abilities? Are you starting to feel some changes happening around you?

It would be easy to think that you're going crazy or sometimes things are just not making sense. Well, you are not alone! All of the above are just a few of the things that drive me and those around me crazy and I am here to tell you that the more psychic you get the crazier it can feel.

In this book, I am hoping to introduce you to some of the many levels of development I have experienced and wasn't aware of at the time. Sometimes, you don't know you are going through something until you have been through it. You might find that you can relate to some of my experiences, gain an insight and a further understanding that helps you identify where you are on your spiritual journey, and it leads to further exploration. No one knows for sure how long the path is. It appears to be infinite.

I do know that this can be an exciting time. You might be a little bit nervous, apprehensive and looking for reassurance. You might have trust issues, lack confidence and are not sure if you believe in yourself, or you could be still in denial as you are surrounded by sceptics that have never encouraged you.

In my teaching experience, I have found that everyone develops at a different pace and has their own individual, intuitive gifts. As

Preface

you develop more skills and confidence, the pace can speed up. I am here to help you develop an understanding as you navigate through the different levels on your way. You may not know where you are on your journey, but be reassured that you are actually on a journey and it can be affirming to know that you are heading in the right direction.

By buying this book, you have already started the journey of choosing to develop your psychic abilities and awareness. However you may have come across this book, it is no accident. This is a sign that some call serendipity.

When a new student comes to my academy to learn to develop their psychic abilities, I warn them that their psychic gift or abilities are much like a 'muscle', and if you don't use that muscle it will be weak and flaccid. Everyone is psychic, but not everyone uses that muscle or chooses to use it. If your arm was in a plaster cast and tied down for six months or longer, the muscles in your arm would have deteriorated and atrophied due to lack of use and may not respond as well. A bit like the astronauts that go up into outer space where there is zero gravity, and they don't need to use their muscles. When they come back to Earth, I am told their muscles have wasted and they are not as strong. That is what can happen with your psychic muscle; it needs to be used and flexed to get stronger. The more you use it, the stronger and more comfortable and confident you can become. So, the warning is to expect to grow, develop and start to notice the changes in your abilities. The desire is to develop your psychic abilities, and if you have that intention that can and will happen.

Of course, you develop faster if you actually read the book and do the exercises. Remember, do not just leave it on the bedside table, in a bookcase or on the floor.

Imagine that this is a fitness manual, a how-to book, full of exercises to develop your psychic strengths to prepare you for your new career as a professional psychic or an intuitive. The choice is yours as to how far you go. You may choose to develop your gifts to work professionally or just for your own benefit, to have a leading edge. Wouldn't it be good to know when your children are sneaking out of home or up to no good, or to be able to pre-empt a perilous situation before it happens? Whatever your reasons, it will all work better if you get started and then keep going.

For many years, I was floundering around wanting to develop psychically and not knowing who to turn to for help or who to trust with assisting me to get to the next level and beyond. Whilst on this journey, I met many people who were prepared to take my money and offer promises, but did not deliver as their main focus was themselves. I even met teachers who held the students back, as it was not good if you managed to outshine them. I learnt a lot of lessons about what I didn't like in a teacher, and I was then determined to not be that type of tutor. I even had a teacher who was a bully, whose style was to push you hard and have you fearful of making a mistake the whole time. That definitely is not good as most of us empaths are far too sensitive to respond to that sort of treatment, and it can be more detrimental than helpful.

Then I read a book about a student that used to visit a teacher for one-on-one training, and I decided that was what I wanted. I wanted to go to a psychic school to learn in a professional environment. I couldn't find the one-on-one teaching experience, but I did find the Arthur Findlay College of Mediumship in England, with the most amazingly talented tutors, and I have been travelling from Australia to England to attend this college every year for many years.

I made a decision that I wanted to be the teacher who offered one-on-one tutoring. I wanted to provide a nurturing environment where

Preface

students could come, learn and practise their newly developing skills, without fear of ridicule. I wanted to provide a caring and empowering environment where they didn't need to fear making a mistake. I started writing the exercises down, one by one, making the lesson plans that I had been taught to do when I was trained to be a TAFE teacher, and then proceeded to teach these lessons. Guess what? They worked! Of course they did! Soon I had a huge folder full of exercises, that was growing day by day, a teaching plan and students wanting a copy of it, as well as eager to learn more. I kept saying, "Sure, someday I will put them in a book for you." This is that book, and hopefully, the first of many. It not only contains some of the lessons, it also shares some of my experiences along my journey, as well as the proof that they worked. This is it!

After compiling the exercises in my ever-growing manual, I then spent five years teaching them, as well as adding to and modifying them to prove that they worked. From there I produced many self-paced online courses that are available at www.katy-k.thinkific.com. There have been many students whom I have taught from the contents of this book who are now confident teachers, professional psychic readers and mediums. So have faith, for they do work and can work for you. Sit down and absorb the contents of this book, and when you are ready to further explore you might like to check out my website www.katy-k.com where there are many more opportunities to help you to progress on your journey. What are you waiting for? Let's get started!

Introduction: Welcome to the 'Modern Oracle'

It is never too late to be who you might have been
—George Eliot.

You might not know how you came to be reading this book, but rest assured, if you are, then you have already begun your psychic journey and I look forward to being your guide along the way.

Are you looking for direction? Have you started to notice many coincidences or synchronicities that have been happening and wondered why? Are you wondering about the next step, or how to turn on your intuitive gift 24/7? You could be questioning why you know some things and how you can expand on them. What are the 'intuitive tools' and how do I use them? How do I trust what I know? How and where do I start? These are all questions that a lot of people ask themselves and you too may have asked. I know I did! I hope that as you read this book it will answer your questions, and know that there will always be many more questions to come: by questioning we learn.

By choosing to read this book you have made a decision to increase your awareness and further develop your spiritual gifts. You might already be aware that you have a gift. Everyone has a gift, and everyone is psychic, but only some of us choose to acknowledge or believe it. For some they have forgotten how to use it, shut it off due to outside influences or not recognised it at all. We all have intuition; just some of us use it more and are more in touch with it. Some people call it a 'gut feeling', that feeling in your stomach that you have about certain situations or people. Many of us label it in different ways, such as clairvoyant, claircognizant, clairaudient and so on. Whichever category you fall into you are here for the purpose of learning more and assisting the growth of your gifts. Recognising it is the first step.

Did you get that part where I said, "Everyone is psychic?" It is true! Think of it as another ability that you can develop. Consider that it can be as easy for you as it is to move and think, but we all do it at different levels or not at all. Usually, it is fear that holds us back.

Many people are using their psychic gifts from birth and can tell you about growing up being psychic. If this is not you then don't be dismayed. A lot of people have an awakening when they hit their 40s. Some of you may come from a family background of psychics. Some have no psychics in the family gene pool that they are aware of and feel like the odd one out, and also struggle with acceptance. The urge to reawaken or tap into your gifts can happen at any time in your life. There are also a lot of people that are unaware they are working with energy and think everyone else is the same.

Introduction: Welcome to the 'Modern Oracle'

We are all different!

In this book, I cover how to recognise your current gifts and determine what other gifts you may wish to further explore. For example, there is a chapter on animal communication. Have you ever wondered what your pet is trying to tell you? Maybe your pet is already communicating with you and you haven't yet realised it.

I also give you a little peek into my life as a psychic and how I have sought evidence to prove a lot of the unexplainable that we are expected to take at face value.

Over many years, I have had different experiences that I will share with you in this book. A lot of what I share is a culmination of learnings from many sources, including many different tutors worldwide, from readings, personal experiences and channelled information from Spirit. All this has brought me to what I communicate to you in this book.

I am happy that you have made the decision to continue developing with me. I am proud to be your mentor on this part of your spiritual journey and look forward to hearing from you in the future as you celebrate your success. I love hearing from the many psychics I have already mentored and guided over the years to develop further on their path. Many have gone on to become professional working psychics, mediums, teachers and much more than they already were. I am a working psychic as well as a tutor. Having said that, I have never considered what I do to be work as I love doing it and I hope you will too.

This book could be a starting point for you, a reference guide, or maybe it is like a refresher course of information that you have always known deep inside or have learnt along the way. Whichever it is for you I trust that you will enjoy, learn and grow.

The Shutdown

Let no one take your personal power away, and if you do it is never too late to reclaim it
—Kathryn Keenan.

Some might find it hard to believe that anyone would want to shut down their psychic gifts but that is just what I did as a child. Just a few careless, rage-filled words from a loved one were enough for me to shut down, and then it was a long time before my gifts were reawakened. The sad thing was that no one even realised what had happened. I just withdrew into myself and got on with life.

As a child I always had a sense of knowing—not that I knew what I was doing at the time, it was just this feeling I would have about certain things—and being a young child, I did not realise that not everyone would want to hear about what I thought. I have always been direct in my speaking and I imagine as a child, I had yet to learn how to be tactful.

The shutdown event was innocent enough. I had expressed my feeling of warning, only to be told to "Shut up! You're such a bloody know-it-all," and to make it worse it was not the only time that it had happened. I grew to hate being called a know-it-all. It hurt, as I thought I was being caring. I was only doing what I often witnessed my mother doing; she would warn us not to do something to avoid an undesirable outcome. This time, it appears, was the proverbial straw that broke the camel's back. My stepfather (who I called Dad, as he was the only dad I ever knew) was over it, and passionately blasted me with great anger, and with that my feelings were well and truly hurt. I was so sensitive that I took the incident to heart and there and then I decided to do as he said as I did not feel appreciated. Without knowing what I was doing, I shut down those feelings and thoughts. This was the catalyst that led to the decision to never tell him anything again, as I sulked in my sadness. I finally got his message and those few words had a devastating effect on me.

My dad, Barry, was a civil engineer, with a very logical brain. His idea of fun was to do mathematical equations and encourage anyone that would engage with him to participate. Not my idea of fun! We could not have been any more different. Dad with his analytical brain and me with my creative one. I was brought up to feel grateful that he had taken on a ready-made family when he took on my sister Linda and I. The conditioning was to never ask for anything, to not be a burden, and that we should be grateful. I know my dad didn't see us as any different to the two children he went on to father. I realised later in life that this came from my orphaned mother's own childhood conditioning. Then, on the other hand, Mum's desire for unity in the family led to much secrecy of the fact that my younger sister Linda and I had a different biological father, Kevin. He was never spoken

The Shutdown

of when I was a child. We were raised with my dad's surname; back then you rarely had to produce a birth certificate. It wasn't until I needed a passport as an adult that I saw my birth certificate. It was then decided to change my name by deed poll, to further keep the secret. It took until the day I got married for my mother to talk a bit about Kevin; she never wanted to offend our 'dad' Barry.

Now, no longer using my unappreciated psychic gift, that muscle had deteriorated over time. It weakened until it was just a thing of the past. Dad never meant me any harm; he was just over being 'told' by a child.

I still had a raging interest and I remember having a young friend who had recently emigrated from Korea, whose grandmother had taught her how to read palms. One day when she was visiting my home, she read my mother's palm with great accuracy and then she read mine. I was fascinated and remember desiring to be able to read palms with such great accuracy. Her impact had impressed me so much that as an adult I went on to study palmistry. I am currently the owner of more than 55 books on palmistry and now teach it.

I now know that it was probably a blessing that I did shut down, especially as I navigated my teenage years, as it ensured that I didn't become an oddity and ostracised by others that feared or didn't understand. The woo-woo was not as easily accepted then as it is now.

My gift started to reignite after I married my husband Tony (a very logical policeman) when I was in my twenties. I had not let on that I had a psychic gift, nor had I discussed anything woo-woo with him.

My mother would every now and then say that she knew something (a premonition) because she was psychic; she was claiming recognition. My cheeky husband would humour her and agree, not wanting to get her offside. He had this harmless little joke whenever my mother,

Maria, would mention how psychic she was. He would chuckle and say to me, when he knew no one could hear him, "You mean 'psycho'!" He was not trying to be mean; he just couldn't get his head around it and dealt with the situation with humour. That was enough for me not to show my hand, until the day I could no longer hide it from him.

As my psychic gift was re-emerging, I was always worried I would look stupid or crazy if I 'got it wrong'. Yes, I know that is ego talking, but I didn't trust my gift. This is very common when people are first opening up and a big fear that my students often state.

I recall one of the first incidents where I was nearly found out was when we were living on Thursday Island and newlyweds. Tony was the only detective up there at that time. He would sometimes talk about his work, but never divulge anything confidential. One day I unthinkingly commented with accuracy about a police issue only for him to ask if I had been reading the police files thinking he might have brought one home, which he rarely did, and angrily telling me that I am not allowed to read them. I had never read any police files! I had to do a lot of backtracking to talk my way out of that situation. He was starting to become suspicious as I was 'still in the closet', as one of my friends would say years later. I had a way of dropping guidance into a conversation and manipulating it to look like they had mentioned it previously. I wasn't ready to 'come out' and show my hand, as I was in no way confident in my skills at that point in time. The worry of getting it wrong was what kept me in the closet for a long time. I am sure many of you also worry about getting it wrong too.

Another time, Tony was to fly to Melbourne from Thursday Island for a court case. I had a strong feeling that he would not be going, and I mentioned my feelings to him. I got away with it as he thought I was just saying that because I didn't want him to go. Tony flew out; however, he only got as far as Cairns before he was told to come back

The Shutdown

as the court case had been put on hold. It seemed the criminal had got a mate to shoot him in the buttocks while he was jogging and was now in hospital; apparently jogging was not something this person usually did. Tony was so disappointed as he had really been looking forward to going to Melbourne as the flights were so expensive, and we could only afford to leave the island once a year.

There were many more incidents similar to this, as my gift was now getting stronger and stronger. We only had one TV channel, there was no YouTube or google back then, and I did not have access to spiritual books on that isolated Island. There was no one else talking about anything woo-woo and there was no way I could learn more about my spiritual gifts to be able to understand them more. I didn't know how I knew things, or received the information, I just did.

What did blow my cover was a family road trip to my parents' house in Gladstone so they could meet their new grandson. Our son, John, was only a few months old, and Chloe was three and a half years old. At that time, it was a long, boring eight-hour trip with not much to see, not a lot of traffic and we were in the middle of nowhere, travelling at the speed limit of 100 km/hr. Tony was driving and listening to his music, a CD that I wasn't a fan of. The children were sleeping, and I was engrossed in a book. All of a sudden, I felt a chill, the hair stood up on my arms and I stopped reading as a vision popped into my head. It was so real and like watching a video recorded on time lapse. I saw our car going up an incline on this two-way highway and ahead of us was a car parked in the middle of the lane we were travelling on. Beside it, off-road, was a car parked parallel to it. As it was not a busy highway, they probably thought they would get away with it as they chatted, or they were just plain stupid. Coming in the other direction was another car travelling at high speed. In my vision there was nowhere to go and unless we did something we were going to crash.

I didn't stop to think as I said with great emotion and fear, "Tony, slow down!" I then proceeded to rapidly explain that our car was going to crash if he didn't, followed by what I thought was going to happen once we got over the incline.

He replied, "I can't, there is someone coming up behind us."

"Slow down or we are going to crash," I yelled. He started braking to slow down. When we got to the top of the incline the scene in front of us was exactly as I had described. Tony started rapidly flashing his lights at the oncoming car. Luckily the driver was alert and veered off the road as much as he could. Tony then managed to steer our car between the parked car in our lane and the oncoming car safely. An accident had been averted.

My vision had prevented a catastrophe; the car behind us had slowed down too and therefore he didn't run into the rear of our car, where our beautiful babies were sleeping. "We were lucky we didn't lose our mirrors," Tony said after a lot of cursing. All the defensive driving training he had done at the police academy had paid off. When we arrived at my parents' place Tony recounted the tale of our near miss and was grateful that his defensive driving skills had saved our lives.

"Yes, you were amazing, and we were lucky that I was able to warn you in time," I added.

Then my mother proudly piped up with, "You're lucky that she is psychic like me!" My cover was blown.

Not long after that incident, we went for a short trip to Daydream Island. We decided to go for a walk and explore as I was trying to lose the baby fat I had acquired during my pregnancy. We put the children in the crèche to be looked after and off we went. We were

The Shutdown

not far into our walk when Tony asked, "These voices you hear, are they actual voices or thoughts?"

"They are thoughts," I replied.

With a deep sigh of relief, he said, "Thank God for that. I thought you were going crazy and I would have to get you locked up." Meaning treatment in a psych ward.

"You would not dare," I angrily replied.

"I would if you are delusional, and your reply was that they were real voices. I have had to do that before."

With indignation I replied, "Are you serious? You would not, why would you even say that?"

He replied, seriously, "I deal with crazies all the time and that is what happens." He was somewhat relieved and questioned me further. He was very good at interrogation as that was a skill he used in his job. I was relieved as I didn't have to hide my gifts from him anymore.

It is very easy to doubt yourself, especially if you don't have anyone to support you. Not everyone has the support and encouragement they need. In this chapter you have learnt from my story that you are not the only one with doubts and fears. If you don't believe in yourself, how can you expect anyone else to? I certainly didn't believe in myself after being shut down as a child, and I certainly didn't decide when it was time to reactivate my gifts. The choice was taken out of my hands as the energy kept building stronger and stronger, and so did the feeling that something was missing in my life.

When something is missing it is human nature to look for what is missing. My feeling of discontent kept growing. It was only appeased a little when I interacted in the metaphysical world. Synchronicities kept happening which would guide me to be in the right place at the right time as opportunities were presented. There was a feeling of rightness and excitement as they did. The right people that were like-minded were coming into my life and they would end up guiding me further on my journey of development.

I encourage you to keep a dedicated psychic journal where you can record all the weird and unexplainable experiences that happen on your journey, as well as any other learnings. There are more suggestions in the following exercise ('Keeping a Psychic Journal') that can help you to track your progress.

Keeping a Psychic Journal

Objective: To journal about the different stages of your development.

Contents of Journal:

This is all about you and your experiences that can include the following:
- Waking thoughts—can be a song
- Dreams—good or bad
- Feelings
- Fears and blocks that you are experiencing
- Anticipations and expectations
- Visions or premonitions
- Thoughts
- Messages received
- Meditations
- Synchronicities
- Symbols and their meanings

When you're hoping to develop your psychic abilities, it is important to journal about the different stages of your development. We soon forget the lessons we learn and the experiences we have. In this journal you will write down any experiences you have, any synchronicities you notice. This journal will help to build your confidence, a record of how far you have come. If you are feeling blocked, anxious or fearful, writing about it will be beneficial; put all your fears in the journal so that they don't block your progress. When you are successful, write about it as it is good to look back at these moments whenever doubt starts to creep in.

Exercise: Recording Your Insights

Five minutes of silent meditation.
Close eyes and breathe deeply three times. Relax your mind and body. Notice everything. The thoughts that come into your head, what you smell, how you feel, what you see. Open your eyes and record your experience in your journal.

What did you see?

_____

_____

_____

_____

_____

Keeping a Psychic Journal

What did you think about?

_____

_____

_____

_____

_____

_____

How did you feel?

_____

_____

_____

_____

_____

_____

I Want to Be More Psychic!

The goal is not to be better than the other man, but your previous self
—The Dalai Lama.

As the years went by, the feeling that something was missing in my life was getting stronger. Spirit activity was becoming more frequent and there were a lot of unexplainable incidents. This all ramped up even further when I finally started to get serious about developing and understanding my intuitive gifts. I would read a lot of books, go to a lot of psychic expos, always wanting to be in the energy. The spiritual energy was addictive and exciting. Like a feeling of coming home that my soul seemed to identify. I was finding that doors were being opened and opportunities presented to be with like-minded people to constantly absorb as much information as I could. I was always purchasing different oracle and tarot decks. Many didn't gel with me and were then discarded. I could not walk past a crystal shop without checking it out, often taking home a few crystals. You can imagine how they amassed over the years. This is how I ended up with what Tony likes to refer to as the 'rock quarry'.

I always had this feeling that there had to be more. I was on a journey to become more psychic, to become more powerful and awaken what I had shut down. I didn't want to be average, I wanted to be extraordinary. I wanted to realise my full potential and then go further, so I was constantly seeking self-improvement.

I would read any spiritual book that I could get my hands on. I read a lot of autobiographies by well-known psychics about how they developed on their journey. A pattern that was starting to become obvious was that quite a few of them had suddenly become more psychic after a 'blow to the head'.

I remember being in my car, stopped at the traffic lights, listening to an audio book, where yet another psychic had received a blow to the head and consequently became more psychic. At that moment I thought to myself, *That is what I need, a blow to the head and then it will be like a light bulb turning on.* Wow, how silly and naive I was.

From that point on, over time, I went on to have three blows to the head and I don't think it made any difference at all except to scare my family. I remember falling down a flight of stairs when I was unwell, and waking up in a different room, after being knocked unconscious. Poor Tony, who did not want to leave my side, had carried me there to get a phone and call an ambulance.

I Want to Be More Psychic!

Another time, I head-butted a heritage building in England after tripping over a double-edged gutter in the rain (we don't have them in Australia). Then there was the time I tripped into a hole in Tulum, Mexico, when walking through a tunnel at a sacred site. That too shocked Tony as one minute he was taking a photo while walking behind me and the next minute I was on the ground. Well, you get the picture; if a blow to the head was going to be effective, I had accidentally manifested many opportunities. Did I become more psychic from all those head knocks? Who knows? I really don't believe I did. I have found that my spiritual growth was subtle; I just stayed on the journey hoping I was going in the right direction. I do know that it is different for everyone. I also told the Universe that I didn't want any more blows to the head. So far so good!

I was always looking for a teacher. I had read a book where the author had attended one-on-one psychic tutoring and I wanted that, but I never did find anyone that offered that. So, instead I took any opportunity that presented itself to attend many workshops held by famous and popular psychics and mediums. I learnt many modalities and different forms of healing, including becoming a Reiki master. I was growing stronger as time went by, yet I still felt there was so much more to learn. When I would attend a workshop, I would never tell them what I could do. I didn't want them assuming that I was experienced. I wanted to learn everything. I needed to understand better, have more clarity and hopefully control. How could I learn to trust my gifts when they seemed so random?

One day when working in my office I went to the kitchen to get a drink. As I walked through our home I could see a spirit sitting outside at our patio table. He looked like a cross between my Uncle John who was living and my husband's uncle who was deceased. So, I was not sure who he was. He kept saying the same thing about travelling and a motorbike and being careful. Although Tony rides a motorbike recreationally, I did not think this was a concern. But I was planning to drive four hours to Brisbane a couple of days later and I wondered if this was a concern. I mentioned this to Tony, and for a sceptic, he was great and said, "How about I book you a flight down on Friday and I will drive down with the children and pick you up on the Sunday?" This was going to suit him well, as there happened to be a boat show at the coast that same day that he wanted to attend and set some goals for himself. Whilst at the boat show we had a phone call from my Uncle John to say that his son was in intensive care after a motorbike accident. He was following a track on his dirt bike and drove over the edge of a cliff and collided with a tree. He was lucky to have survived. Many months later I was visiting my uncle's home and I noticed a photo of his dad. He was the man that I saw sitting at my patio table. I now understood what he was trying to tell me. This left me even more frustrated. There was no sense in receiving warnings if I couldn't interpret them. This was the catalyst for change that motivated me to learn more. The pivot point that ended up being life-changing!

Off to Hogwarts

You don't have to be great to start, but you have to start to be great

—Zig Ziglar.

"First, you're going to connect. Then I want you to start with their gender, their age, when they died, their relationship to me, what they did, their career, how they died, a shared memory known to me, give a message and then close. Oh, and since I know a lot of people in spirit, there is no need for the same person to come through twice."

Oh my God, what had I gotten myself into? I didn't know how to get started, what closing was, or whether I could bring through the shopping list of information needed for validation. I also wondered if I could sneak out without anyone noticing. Unfortunately, there was no chance of that. This was my very first visit to the Arthur Findlay College, the realisation of a dream.

The idea for attending the Arthur Findlay College had come to me in a random way. I had asked my guides to find me a teacher that could guide me further so I could get a handle and understanding of my psychic gifts, as well as to show me the way forward. I needed more guidance. I wanted a teacher that could help me deal with this nagging feeling of incompleteness. A feeling of there has to be more, but I didn't know what. At that stage of my experience, I had no understanding of the difference between a psychic or a medium. I thought that everything I did was classified as being a psychic.

I was standing near my bookshelf looking for a particular book when a book literally jumped off the shelf and landed open at my feet. As I picked up the book, I noticed the page it was open at was about the author of the book attending the Arthur Findlay College of Mediumship at Stansted Hall in England. I had enjoyed reading this particular book years ago but had no recollection of reading this chapter. I guess I wasn't ready at that time. As I read through the pages, my excitement grew, and I knew that this was what I wanted to do. I had found the next step! Now to convince my family of the value of attending this college and that I would be safe. No, I wasn't going off to join a cult that would take advantage of me.

An internet search soon provided knowledge of the courses that were available, and the tutors. As I didn't know of them, I really didn't know what I was getting into. All I knew was I had to go and then maybe they could help 'sort' me out! Work out how to handle my gifts and show me how to use them better and what I could do with them.

It ended up that choosing the time of year to go and the right tutor was all left up to chance. There were only two gaps that were long

Off to Hogwarts

enough in our calendar. I asked my muggle (a person who is not conversant with a particular activity or skill) husband to choose which option would be the most suitable, timewise. The option that would allow me to get away for two weeks at the college (plus travel time and jetlag days), because if I was going to travel that far, I was going to go for two weeks. Luckily, he chose the option I wanted that interested me the most.

This was going to be my first ever overseas trip on my own, and I found that daunting. I mean, to get there I had to travel all the way from Australia to England, leaving my loving family behind. I had concerns of leaving Tony to juggle work and look after our two teenage children, who I hoped would not run amok, while I was not there keeping a close eye on them. You don't get away with a lot when your mother is psychic!

I put a lot of pressure on myself to make this trip worthwhile as a lot of sacrifices were made for me to even get to England. I didn't want to put any extra pressure on our budget and told Spirit I would only go if I could finance the trip through my readings. Then I became busy with an influx of people who had heard about me through a friend of a friend; I took it as a sign Spirit wanted me to go. It was not long before I was on a plane headed for England.

I remember the first time I went to the Arthur Findlay College of Mediumship. I was terrified! There was a strong fear of failure after spending a fortune to travel to the other side of the world as well as the cost of attending this prestigious college. I needed to succeed and grow after such an investment.

Once I had arrived and settled in, I attended an interview with a tutor to see where and who I would be placed with. Unbeknown to me at that time, when students book these courses the majority are wanting to be with the course co-ordinator, so the interview becomes a time to impress him and get into his class! The tutor asked whether I was 'beginners' or 'intermediate' (the two levels offered). I said I didn't know. I mean, how do you measure yourself? I didn't even know if I should have been there! I was so nervous. At that point he looked over my shoulder then back at me several times and stated, "You will be in intermediate and I will meet you in the library at 3:00 p.m." There was nothing calming about his manner and he promptly dismissed me and called the next student over.

I entered the library at 3:00 p.m. to find all the chairs in a circle and students quickly finding seats. There were 14 chairs, not including the tutor's, and I chose a seat as far from the tutor's as possible. Then came the process of each student having to give a demonstration in front of everyone. Fear was starting to take hold as each student was chosen to demonstrate. His impatient comments were not helping either.

"Come on, who have you got here? It is not hard! Is it a male or a female? You have all been chosen to be in this class because either you think you're intermediate level or I know you are, so show me what you can do. And you should be working faster than this. Now hurry up and get your link!"

There was a lot of pressure on me to make this trip worthwhile. My husband and children were at home managing without me. Sacrifices had been made so I could travel all the way to England. Sneaking out of my first class wouldn't have been ideal. I watched as the other students struggled. It seemed many of them had been in this class many times before, and I thought, *He must be a good teacher* ... right? After an hour and a half of stomach-churning fear—and I was not the only one—we were sent on our break for the evening meal. The rest of us were to continue demonstrating after dinner, which gave me even more time to fret and worry.

Off to Hogwarts

When we returned the tutor decided it was my turn. I stood up, determined that being kicked out and sent home before I learnt anything would be the worst thing that could possibly happen. I walked to the spot beside his seat, closed my eyes, said a prayer and saw nothing! My fear started to escalate.

"Come on, we haven't got all night. It's easy. You either have a male or a female. Which is it? You have a fifty-fifty chance of getting it right!"

I opened my eyes and without thinking said, "A male."

"Okay," he drawled. "So who is he?"

"He says he is like a grandfather to you, but he isn't."

"Either he is or he isn't. Which is it?" he questioned.

"I can't change it, that's what he is saying," I replied boldly. I was past the fear stage and about to give up so had nothing to lose!

"Well, let's see where you're going with that!" he replied.

I closed my eyes and said to my guides, "Please, help me. You have to give me something more than this, or I'm out of here!"

Then I felt the right side of my body start to droop as if I had had a stroke. Pictures started flooding my mind and the words flowed, meeting the shopping list of information we were supposed to gather to prove the existence of life after death. I felt like I was disengaged from the rest of the class and it was just me, the grandfather figure and no one else. I could feel his aches, memories and feelings, as if I had stepped into his shoes.

When the words stopped flowing the tutor asked me what the message was, and I delivered it.

"Right, you can sit down now."

Is that all you're going to say after all that? I thought. I boldly turned towards my tutor and asked, "Do you know him?"

"Yes," he replied in a quiet voice, and went on to say he could relate to everything. I smiled and said a silent thank you to the spirit and my guides. I wondered how I had done it and whether I could do it again.

That week was like a baptism of fire. It pushed me out of my comfort zone and showed me so much of what I was capable of. At the end of the week the tutor pulled me aside and asked if I would be coming back in November for his advanced course. I cheekily asked, "Do you think I am ready for that?"

"Yes, I will see you in November," he replied, grinning, as he looked me in the eye.

"Well, that depends on my husband," I said.

"What has it got to do with him?" he asked.

"He pays the bills," I said. I then walked away as he had no answer to that.

I thought I had had enough, but he knew I would be back. Those two weeks were just the beginning.

Fast forward 15 years and I have made many annual visits to the Arthur Findlay College and studied with many different tutors. Each tutor has their own style. No matter what I thought at the time, that first tutor was right for me and got the best out of me. I will be eternally grateful, but I then moved on to tutors that were gentler and made it more fun.

The shopping list approach has softened. Most tutors now encourage a more personal experience where the client should feel the presence of their loved one, as if they are in the room with them and the information is more natural. Yes, the details of the loved one's life are important, but so is the genuine experience. The focus is now on bringing through the essence of the spirit and the love they want to express with personal memories and messages.

Psychics in the Family Tree

We are all gifted. That is our inheritance
—Ethel Waters.

Questions I get asked a lot are, "Are there any other psychics in your family?" and "Were you born with your gifts?"

My 'gifts', you could say, are in my genes on both sides of the family tree and it appears that there are a lot of 'branches' that have contributed to my intuitive gifts.

I didn't get to meet my father's family until I was in my forties, and prior to that I couldn't work out why my gifts were so different to my mother's.

The Modern Oracle

I don't have any memories of my dad Kevin, as he tragically died when he was 21 years of age, and I was only 15 months old. He was on his way to the hospital to be with my mother while she gave birth to my sister Linda, and he had a fatal car accident. So, therefore, I didn't know a lot about him. But I have since discovered that his sister Kathleen was a 'working' psychic.

Kevin's father William (my grandfather) was a trance medium and a healer in Brisbane. William was also a member of the Masonic lodge, and he had a doctor friend who believed in William's gift of healing. This doctor would take William to the burns unit at the hospital where he worked, so that William could give healing to his patients. William also had a doctor in spirit, as part of his 'spirit team', and this doctor communicated through William while he was in a trance state, imparting medical advice for people in his audience.

William's mother Myrtle (my great-grandmother) was able to do automatic writing and had doctors in spirit that communicated through her as well. Myrtle's brother was a trance medium, and all of William's six sisters were involved in the spiritual church and gifted in some way.

My mother Maria is a psychic and she had psychics on both sides of her family tree too. Her mother, Katina (my grandmother), was gifted, and I am told that my mother's grandmother (on her father's side) read coffee cups, and people went to her for guidance. Mum's aunty taught her how to read tea and coffee cups. Mum was also very lucky backing horses, a gift I did not inherit.

I recall one day Mum decided to put a bet on some horses. My sister Julianne said, "Whatever horses Mum backs, do the same." We watched Mum fill out a form to place a bet on a trifecta, and we copied her bet. A trifecta is when you back three horses to come in first, second

Psychics in the Family Tree

and third place. We all placed our bet and unbeknown to us, Mum had a funny feeling about the third-placed horse, and went and placed another bet, where she changed the horse she thought would come third. Guess what? Both her bets won, because two horses tied for third place. That was why she had the funny feeling and placed the second bet.

My mother also has vivid, predictive dreams that feel so very real to her. In her dreams her grandmother comes to her to give her warnings. She also communicates with my mother's sister, Ann. You could say that after raising Mum and her siblings their grandmother is still looking out for them. My mother and her siblings became orphaned when my mother was only five years old. Her father died first at age thirty-two and six months later her mother died at the age of twenty-eight, leaving their three children all under the age of ten years orphaned.

You don't have to have had intuitives in your family tree for you to be psychic. You might find that no one else in your gene pool bothered to develop their gifts. A lot of people hide their gift due to a fear of ridicule, they are surrounded by sceptics, they don't feel confident or they are not interested. So, if you think you don't have any psychic kin, be the first one to develop your unique gifts and see what unfolds.

How Do I Know If I Am Psychic?

Discover the truth about your underlying psychic gifts and not only stop thinking of yourself as crazy but also empower yourself to make a major difference in the lives of others

—Catherine Carrigan.

We are all psychic, just some of us choose not to use our psychic gifts. Being psychic is not a rare and special gift that only a few obtain. Under the umbrella of the word 'psychic' there are a multitude of gifts.

The Modern Oracle

In ancient Greek Psyche is as much a name as a word. Psyche means 'the soul' or 'breath of life' or 'mind' and was considered the spiritual part of a human being as opposed to the physical
—Robert Osterman.

Have you ever heard of the sixth sense? Some of you may choose to call it intuition and some of you bundle all your gifts under the label of being psychic.

We use all our five senses without thinking. Our sixth sense works like that too. It is called 'claircognizance', which means 'clear knowing'. The sense of knowing can be described as something that comes to you with certainty, and you don't know how you know, you just know.

Our spiritual senses align with our physical senses and some have more than one name.

The sense of sight is *clairvoyance*—clear seeing.
The sense of touch is *clairsentience*—clear feeling.
The sense of hearing is *clairaudience*—clear hearing.
The sense of smelling is *clairalience* or *clairolfaction*—clear smelling.
The sense of tasting is *clairgustance*—clear tasting.
The sense of knowing is *claircognizance*—clear knowing.

Sometimes we question or doubt our psychic abilities, feeling we need proof or more evidence of our gifts.

On the next page is a list of 'signs' that you may experience on your spiritual journey.
Please note that not everyone will experience all of them, especially as we are all continually evolving.

How Do I Know If I Am Psychic?

There are some common patterns that can happen as we evolve intuitively, and they can act as a tool for determining how psychic you are. You may experience a few signs for some time before you experience many others. The signs may arouse a curiosity, a desire to investigate and learn more to enable you to move forward. Think of your gift as a muscle: the more you use it, the stronger and more confident you can become.

An increase in spiritual activity will not go away and can continue to increase as you work more with your intuition.

Below is a small quiz that can be a guideline to let you know how you are going with your psychic development. Of course, there are many more signs than I have listed, I just don't want to overwhelm you with them all at this point.

You might like to score yourself by counting how many of the 17 signs you ticked and then check back in a few months to see if there have been any changes to the number of boxes you tick. It is not a competition, and it is not necessary to compare yourself to anyone else. We all develop at different rates and sometimes we can have a growth spurt. Have fun!

Am I Psychic?

- ☐ Common coincidences occurring in your life
- ☐ Seeing people or things out of the corner of your eye that are not there when you look around
- ☐ Feeling a 'breeze' or a presence
- ☐ Strong fascination for psychic or spiritual knowledge
- ☐ Receiving 'messages' in dreams from friends or relatives who have died

- ☐ Dreaming of events before they happen
- ☐ Seeing those who are no longer alive
- ☐ People want to tell you their life history and things they have rarely told others, even if they do not know you very well
- ☐ 'Knowing' people well when you have only met them for a short time
- ☐ Sensitivity to noise (loud to others is really loud for you!)
- ☐ Sensitivity to the moods of others. You feel what they feel and mirror them. You can become irritable if they are, as you pick up their energy
- ☐ Fascination with angels or fairies
- ☐ Rubbing the forehead often and wanting to get hair away from your face. A strange pulling sensation across forehead ('third eye' stretching)
- ☐ Increased irritability for some, not all. This is caused by the lack of comprehension of others to respect you and the changes you are experiencing as you develop
- ☐ Intolerance where previously you have been very tolerant
- ☐ Willingness to speak up when previously you have kept quiet
- ☐ Temporarily unreliable, because you are in your 'own world'

What Psychic Gifts Do I Have?

Have you ever wondered what psychic gifts you have?

Some of you might find that you have a dominant gift. As you read the following you might discover which 'sense' is your dominant sense, and which senses you are still to develop further. Not everyone uses all senses. You could be using all of them, but one will be more dominant.

How Do I Know If I Am Psychic?

Clairsentience—Clear Feeling or Sensing

Clairsentients say, *"I feel."*

They pick up on emotions and perhaps events that have happened a long time ago. They are also skilled in psychometry and can pick up impressions left on objects. Clairsentients can also do the following.

- They can pick up if someone is in a bad mood or emotional before they even say a word
- They can be affected by the moods of others around them
- They find it easier to learn by being shown how and then doing
- They feel things when receiving information
- They are often healers

Clairalience and Clairolfaction—Clear Smelling

When the psychic is using this sense they will say, *"I smell."*

This sense is named by two names, and both have the ability to pick up on distinctive smells that are being transmitted by the spirit. Usually no one else around them can smell the odour.

- They smell things when receiving information, such as coffee, smoke, perfume or cologne, burning smells, foods that have a distinctive smell
- They might smell cigarettes or pipe tobacco, when there are no smokers in the room
- Usually, the smell can be related to the spirit who is sending the message, e.g. the perfume that their grandmother wore, the pipe that their grandfather smoked

- Clear smelling is sometimes included under the label of clairsentient

Clairgustance—Clear Tasting

When the psychic is using this sense they will say, *"I am tasting, or I can taste."*

Usually the psychic will 'taste' essences being transmitted by spirit.

- Usually something the spirit loved
- It can identify their workplace; e.g. they worked in a liquorice factory

Clairaudience—Clear Hearing

Clairaudients say, *"I hear."*

They pick up voices, music and sounds that give them psychic insight and can be telepathic.

They can tune into people's thoughts and emotions.

Clairaudients make good mediums and communicate well with spirit. They hear communication as thoughts if subjectively and sound if objectively.

Some sounds they might hear are music, laughter, someone calling their name when no one is there, bells, crying and whispers.

- They learn by listening to a teacher speak, to CDs, to music
- They hear words, sentences or see words in the mind

How Do I Know If I Am Psychic?

Clairvoyance—Clear Seeing

Clairvoyants say, *"I see."*

They are visual. They usually see pictures, symbols, images or mini movies of events in their mind's eye, using their 'third eye' chakra. This also includes dreams.

These images can be about the past, present or future.

Clairvoyants usually have an affinity with tarot or oracle cards and when reading intuitively they use the pictures on the cards as a point of focus to see even more pictures.

- They learn by reading the written word or seeing a picture
- They tend to like wearing bright colours and are conscious of their appearance and sometimes talk quickly
- They interpret symbols

The following are different forms of clairvoyance.

- Seeing auras
- Seeing past lives
- Body scanning
- Visions through dreams
- Seeing spirit entities

Claircognizance—Clear Knowing

This is the ability to know things without being told and to receive fully formed ideas. You just know and feel strongly about this. Nothing can change your mind.

Exercise:

After reading about all the different 'clairs' you might like to answer the questions below. As you develop your spiritual gifts you might like to review this exercise to see what changes have occurred, if any.

Which sense comes naturally to you?

_____

_____

Which sense is your dominant sense?

_____

_____

Which sense is your weakest sense?

_____

_____

Which sense would you like to develop more?

_____

_____

Are you able to work with all your senses when working psychically?

_____

_____

Trust and Belief

Trust in your abilities and never doubt your potential to achieve. No matter how much negativity exists around you, you will have the power to do wonderful, remarkable things
—Siva Sankar Reddy.

Humans are born with only two innate fears: the fear of falling and the fear of loud sounds. Unfortunately, we acquire more fears as we age, and then, we have to learn to trust again to get past our fears and progress. By the time a student comes to me wanting to develop their intuitive gifts, their fears are already ingrained. I, too, was fearful, and my greatest fear was, "What if I get it wrong?" I am sure there are many of you reading this book that have that same fear. It is a huge responsibility if people are going to put their trust in you.

Children trust until they learn from experiences not to trust. Years ago, my sister Julianne's pet dog Jubilee died. Jubilee was well loved and elderly in dog years when he died.

For my nephews Luca (five) and Giorgio (three) it was their first encounter with losing a loved one while being old enough to comprehend the loss.

Each night before their meal they would each say a short prayer to God. When it was Giorgio's turn, he would always say the same thing: "Dear Lord, please give Jubilee water, amen."

He sounded so cute and his belief was so strong that Jubilee was with God, so therefore he was reminding God to look after him now that Jubilee was in his hands. This was especially important to Giorgio, who has a high sense of responsibility. He knew to ask for what he wanted and trusted that it would happen.

We can often make things difficult and complex for ourselves. Children don't! Learn to be as you were as a young child and ask for what you want and trust that you will receive it, but be careful what you ask for as you just might get it! It is also important to tag on "if it is right for me and my highest good".

As I developed my intuitive gifts I had to learn to get past my fears or I would never trust, and without trust there can be no confidence. If you don't believe in you, then how can you expect anyone else to believe in you? No one likes a wishy-washy, vague psychic. A lack of self-belief can hinder your progress.

In the very early days of my development, fear held me back a lot. I could do an impromptu reading on the spot easily as I didn't have time to work myself into a state of anxiety beforehand. As the word

Trust and Belief

got out about me people wanted to book readings and because of my fear I wouldn't commit to them. The main excuse I told myself was that I was guarding my privacy and did not want clients coming to my home. Then I thought, *Spirit won't want to work with me if I don't make myself available. I know I can do this and what is the worst thing that could happen? If the client is not happy, I will apologise and there will be no charge for the reading. No one has been unhappy so far, I trust!* I decided to book the very next person that requested a reading. The next day the phone rang with a request for a reading and I took the booking on the proviso that I went to them. As I put the phone down all this information started coming through into my head and I knew it was for the client, so I wrote it down, even though I could not relate to it.

A couple of days later I prepared myself and armed with a bag of tools (crystals, tarot cards and pendulum), I set off to the client's home to do the reading. I even had a teapot and herbs to make a cup of lemongrass tea when I got there, to help set the mood. I need not have worried as the deceased family came through and I didn't even get around to pulling the tools out of the bag. I started with the notes I had taken after the phone connection and it just flowed. The client was ecstatic. It didn't matter how many readings I did, I still was not trusting my gift and my main fear was that I would get it wrong and disappoint someone.

I asked myself, "You have already done many successful readings, so why would you fear that you can't do it again?" I had to learn to trust in the process and believe that my spirit team wanted to work with me and would always be there for me.

Trust is the most important key or vital ingredient to being psychic and your development.

Why is that? Because most psychic experiences are non-tangible: you can't touch them, they are not physically solid and it is difficult to prove them.

You need to trust your intuition and trust that it is more powerful than your imagination. I have had students admit that they thought it was all in their imagination. Your psychic gift is natural and requires trust for further growth and enhancement. Just like you believe in night and day you need to believe in yourself and trust your abilities.

Many of us don't exactly know how an aeroplane works. How is it possible for a plane to stay in the sky when it weighs more than most things that can't fly? Yet we travel on planes and we trust that they will stay in the sky and get us to our destination safely. We are trusting that we will be safe.

We have to trust that when we are driving a car we will be safe and every other car will stay on their side of the road, and that driver is focused during their journey. Most of the time we will trust until failure occurs. Then we have to find a way to get around the failure and learn to trust again. When you first learn to ride a bike, you could fall down often before you master riding it. Upon your first time falling, you don't just give up or you would never achieve the ability to ride a bike. When developing your psychic gift, it is easy to fail at the first hurdle and leave your confidence shattered rather than get back up and try again. It is important to keep trying. Even though you may not understand how your gifts work you have to trust that they do.

When I was a young teenager, my beautiful 14-year-old cousin Abigail was tragically killed in a car accident. Her family was travelling home from an event where she was performing successfully in a drama competition when suddenly the onward travelling car veered from the opposite lane of the highway and crashed into their car. The young lady driving the other car had lost control due to a mechanical fault with the steering, and therefore she could not prevent what happened. Some of Abigail's family were seriously injured. It was a very sad time for everyone. Our family was celebrating Dad's birthday when we received the news. There was a feeling of shock and it was hard to believe that she was actually gone.

A week later a big four-wheel-drive car careered into the side of our family car that I was a passenger in, sending it spinning out of control from the impact. The two events had left me fearful of travelling in cars. I no longer trusted that I would be safe. There was no control. It took time for me to eliminate that fear and not feel anxious when I travelled in a car, and to trust that I was going to be safe. I had to keep travelling in cars to build my confidence again.

Fear is the opposite of trust. Fear can shut us down and disable our gifts. Fear is a barrier to reaching our full potential as a psychic. It is okay, though, to feel the fear and use that energy. You can feel the fear and then let it go. Think positively, and about what could go right rather than what could go wrong.

Until we admit our fears, or list them down so we can face them, we don't totally know what we are dealing with. You might like to try the following exercise.

Exercise:

In your dedicated psychic journal write a list of all your fears that could prevent or hinder your development. I have listed a couple of examples that may even be some of your fears.

"What if I get it wrong?"
"What if I am not as good as someone else I know or have heard of?"

Now write in your journal what beliefs you have that could hinder your development. Here are some examples to guide you:

"It has to be genetic and I don't appear to have anyone else in the family tree with an intuitive gift."
"You have to have a blow to the head to open up your gifts or develop at a faster pace."
"My family or partner are non-believers and therefore not supportive."

Many students are held back from further development by a lack of self-confidence. The worry that they have to impress others and then won't be able to. The more experience you have the more self-confident you will be. It is easy to have your confidence shattered, and allow yourself to grind to a halt or shut down. Pay no heed to other people's opinions; everyone has different beliefs. Also, not everyone is going to be of the same opinion. The only person that has to believe in you is you. Believe in yourself and your gift. Let go of any belief that prevents your growth and then create new beliefs.

Exercise:

I want you to think of what empowering beliefs you can have, then write your new empowering beliefs in your psychic journal. These are the new stories you will tell yourself. Sometimes they can be desires of how you would like to be. They should be positive affirmations. See examples below.

"I am a powerful and accurate psychic."
"I trust in my abilities."
"I love and approve of myself."

Trust and Belief

The more you live by and trust in your intuition, the easier it is to make the right decisions and then the easier life becomes. Now do the following exercise to anchor in your new beliefs and affirmations.

Anchoring in Your New Beliefs

1. Close your eyes.
2. Take three deep, long breaths and exhale each one slowly.
3. Relax your body. Tense each part of your body and release the tension.
4. Think of something that really scares you, that you are fearful of from the list in your journal. Go into the fearful energy, the feeling of anxiousness from what you have written should you be in each situation.
5. What does it feel like? Note that it is not an empowering energy. In fact, this energy should feel at the least uncomfortable. Imagine that you have disappointed others with your insights, e.g. the fear of getting it wrong during a reading. Not a good feeling.
6. Now think of something that makes you feel peaceful, something you love. It could even be a cute puppy or kitten, or good chocolate … yum. Anything that makes you feel good.
7. While in this peaceful, joyous and loving energy, anchor your new beliefs. Say them out loud, with passion, and repeat them ten times or more until you believe what you say.
8. Feel that you believe in these new beliefs.
9. Feel powerful.
10. Say them with confidence.
11. Take another deep breath and be aware of your surroundings.
12. Now open your eyes.

The Modern Oracle

It is good to repeat this exercise any time you need a confidence boost. I repeat my new empowering beliefs repeatedly when I swim or walk or anytime I need a boost, and I am constantly adding to my list of phrases.

I have a student that has been training with me for quite a while. She also is a huge fan of and sells *The Modern Oracle* deck and *The Modern Oracle of Essential Oils* deck. Like me, she has to believe in something to sell it and she loves both decks, especially *The Modern Oracle of Essential Oils* deck, as she also sells essential oils and is passionate about aromatherapy.

She started off asking people who came to her market stand to pull a card from *The Modern Oracle of Essential Oils* deck, with the intention of discovering which essential oil would benefit them most. She would then offer them a sample of that oil mixed with a carrier oil in a roller ball bottle for a minimal price. As her confidence grew, she decided to promote a choice of a three-card reading for $20 with the sample oil. She charged according to her belief that no one would pay any more than that. She initially started out doing the reading for free to demonstrate the cards. The more readings she did the more her confidence increased.

I encouraged her to raise her price for the readings because she wasn't valuing her time; the readings would take more than twenty minutes on average. "If you don't value your time, no one else will either," I said. People were also taking advantage of her generous nature and would ask more than one question and that is why she was spending so much time on each reading.

I advised her that there are people out there who will take advantage of you and keep pushing for more but not pay anything additional unless you ask for it. She actually had one customer approach her

Trust and Belief

and shared that she wasn't sure if she wanted a three-card reading, she wanted a more in-depth reading. Again, she offered a free draw of a card to highlight the reading she could offer. The customer was enthralled, asked for more guidance and was ecstatic by the end of the reading. With her confidence growing she was learning to trust in the cards and her ability, but more importantly to value her time and efforts.

One day she called me to tell me that she was asked a difficult question and she was worried about getting it wrong. "So, what did you do?" I asked.

Her reply was, "I decided to trust whatever the cards showed and just say it." She was stunned when the answer brought the client to tears. Over time I kept encouraging her to raise her prices and as her confidence grew, she finally did.

The Modern Oracle decks are a tool that helps you to develop and trust in your abilities because they are so easy to interpret, but like any tool they are only as good as the person wielding it. With practice comes skill.

When you are thinking that you can't or won't be able to develop further, when frustration sets in because you feel you are not progressing fast enough, or you feel your goal is not attainable, think of the following. It was once believed that it was impossible for anyone to run a mile in four minutes, until Roger Bannister did. From then on, many others did too. You can break through the barriers to achieve what you desire; you just have to believe you can do it and then do it. Believe in you.

Trust Your Intuition

Sometimes I nearly drive my husband crazy! I had been receiving messages from my spirit team that there was something wrong with my car tyres. I mentioned it to Tony, and he had a look and couldn't see a problem. Yet, I still had that strong feeling that wouldn't go away. I mentioned it again and he checked the tyres again and still couldn't find a problem. So, to keep me happy, he took my car into a tyre place to get the tyres checked and they too said there was nothing wrong. I was especially worried because I was going to be driving to Brisbane in a few days' time for a healing workshop.

The bad feeling about my tyres was still there. I drove to Brisbane and on some parts of the highway the speed limit is 110 kmph (68 mph). The next day, on the day of the workshop, I heard in my mind, *You better leave early if you want to be on time.*

Of course, most people would say that is just common sense. But this was an hour and a half before the event, and it was only a thirty-minute drive at the most.

I felt this sense of urgency to get going and set off early. I was driving in a 50 km lane and suddenly saw a big flash of bright white light, the size of a person, up ahead in a tree. I heard in my mind, *Slow down*, and as I did, I heard a big bang. My tyre had blown. Luckily, I was going slow enough to pull over to the side of the road; mind you, it was the only place on the whole trip that had a bike riding lane that I could pull over to out of the busy traffic.

I thought, with horror, *I am so lucky*; imagine if my tyre had blown yesterday when I was on the highway driving at 110 kmph. I doubt if I would still be here! I called Tony and said, "You know how I have

Trust and Belief

been worried about my tyres? Well, one of them just blew as I was driving along, and I am going to have to change it."

"No way!" he exclaimed. "It is far too dangerous for you to do in peak hour traffic. Call the RACQ; that is what we pay them for."

I called the RACQ and said a little prayer that they would get to me fast. I really expected to be on the side of the road for at least an hour as they battled the traffic. I then called the co-ordinator of the workshop and as I was explaining what had happened, surprisingly an RACQ car pulled up behind my car. It turns out he was nearby and had just finished another job. I was amazed! Upon inspecting the tyre, a split was found on the inner side. He exclaimed that the tyre was a ticking time bomb and he couldn't believe that it hadn't blown before this. No wonder my guides were so insistent. With my tyre changed I arrived five minutes before the workshop was to start. Not only did my spirit team warn me, but they also protected me, and I truly believe that the flash of light that caused me to slow down was in fact my guardian angel. Here was proof of direct and accurate communication with my spirit team.

You Are Unique!

Try not to get lost in comparing yourself to others. Discover your gifts and let them shine!
—Jennie Finch.

Would you believe that I once had performance anxiety? I would get so anxious before having to demonstrate my skills of mediumship or conduct a reading that I would consider cancelling. At that time, I thought I was the only one. Many of my peers appeared to be very confident and their work seemed effortless. I was comparing myself to others and this did not help my confidence in any way at all. I had thoughts that I was not as good as them. I now know that this is a very common feeling amongst many other psychic mediums.

I have had amazing tutors admit that they too still can get performance anxiety. To see them work you would never believe it. I have a friend who is a well-known psychic and she would often cancel or reschedule due to anxiety, but when I looked at her she seemed so confident. I would often compare myself to others thinking they had it all together. By comparing myself to them, I was actually taking away my own confidence and projecting that I would never be good enough.

Comparing yourself to others can drive your behaviour. Yes, you could strive to be like someone else, which could result in motivating you to achieve or it might just make you feel inadequate and incapable. Comparison can be both motivating and destructive.

You are unique! Your focus and energy would be better served placed on what you are capable of now and how you could improve, rather than comparing your weaknesses to others' strengths. That will not build your confidence, and without confidence it is hard to progress.

Falling into the trap of comparing yourself to others can take away your power, as you may start to believe that you are not good enough. We all develop at a different rate with different strengths, so there really is no comparison to be made. Developing your spiritual gifts is not a competition.

Just like not everyone gets to perform at the Olympics, those that do have different levels of skills and will compete in different areas. It is the same in the spiritual world. You would not compare an Olympic swimmer with an Olympic runner. They are both Olympians, but the swimmer would not be able to run to Olympic levels and nor would the runner be able to swim at Olympic standards. That is why you shouldn't compare yourself to other psychics. Everyone has their own strengths, from the psychic intuitive to the clairsentient, or even a clairvoyant.

As with most things in life, no matter how good we are, we can always be better and improve as well as maintain the new levels we achieve.

You Are Unique!

This happens through determination and practice. Once you get past the battle between your logical thought processes, your deeper intuition and psychic ability can come to the forefront. Your sixth sense can emerge stronger and you will overcome the desire to keep it quiet.

I have found that the best way to develop is to learn new skills and practise. If you don't practise how can you become more confident? There are many psychics who allow their ego to get in the way and think that people will think less of them if they attend a beginner's course or workshop. They may fear that they will no longer be seen as the 'expert'. Progressive masters in their field of expertise will always be wanting to improve or offer something better. No matter what field you are in there is always something to learn.

Take, for example, a singer. There are people who are born with a beautiful singing voice, but they will still benefit from lessons to protect their voice, learn breathing techniques, and learn all about music to enable them to write and/or understand it. This may take years to develop and lots of training and practice. Can you see where I am going with this? The development of your psychic gift will take time and practice. Your aim should be to never stop improving and seeking to learn. I often go to seminars and courses seeking improvement and never assume that I know everything. I believe that you can always continue to grow. Even if you are covering information that you already know, it serves as a timely reminder to 'use it or lose it'.

We have all heard of amazing psychics that have gifts that have led them to becoming famous for their gifts (just like Olympians) and many of us think that it would be good to be able to do what they do. I know that I get star struck and love watching how other psychics and mediums work. I would even call myself a spiritual junkie. I love everything spiritual and metaphysical.

That is why I love going to psychic expos, where I can be in that 'special' energy, surrounded by crystals and all things psychic. It is a real treat for me as I get to be with like-minded people, exploring all that is out there and new developments and techniques, while catching up with others in the industry. I would really recommend you attend a psychic expo if you ever get the chance.

The very important thing to know is to not compare yourself to anyone else. As difficult as it can be not to, there is always going to be someone who is perceived as better or works differently. How good someone is can be an opinion and if you continually compare yourself to others, it can have the potential to hold you back. I have had students that always think they are not good enough due to comparing themselves to others and that is what has prevented them from progressing or even having a go. It is quite common to have these feelings and to be always feeling like the 'new kid on the block'. Many times I have felt like this and I have found the way that worked best for me was to sit quietly, listen, learn and then there were no expectations about my abilities, just surprises when they saw me work. The other benefit is hopefully they won't assume that you already know something or feel intimidated.

There could always be someone that we perceive is more psychic. The idea is to get past that perception; ignore it. Keep moving forward, flex your intuitive muscle and continue to put what you learn into practice. Before you know it you will be surprising yourself and everyone else.

There were many times in the early days of my development where I felt intimidated by what I thought were my lack of skills. It seemed to me that everyone was better than me, so it was easier to lay low.

I was in awe of the celebrity psychics and put them on high pedestals, only to learn that everyone does it a different way. I would attend a class and sit there quietly while others were eager to impress. This actually worked for me as I learnt more by listening. I liked staying under the radar which was due to my lack of confidence. I mean, how could I get it wrong if I didn't participate and wasn't prepared to make a mistake; mistakes were the lessons I learnt from and helped me to progress. I am not suggesting you look to make an error, just learn from them and other people's mistakes.

It was a huge step for me to take when I decided to accept payment for my readings. I felt that if I wasn't as good as I perceived others to be, how could I charge for what I did? Then I realised I had to start somewhere, and I had to gain experience to be experienced. If you are finding yourself having the same thoughts, then you might like to start with charging a minimal amount so that there is an exchange of energy. It is important that there is an exchange of energy, so that your energy isn't depleted. In the beginning I had people exchange for haircuts, healings, massages, crystals, essential oils, gifts and testimonials regarding their reading. Then I progressed to a minimal amount and as the demand grew the price went up.

Validation of Meditation

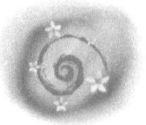

Meditation is like a gym in which you develop the powerful mental muscles of calm and insight

—Ajahn Brahm.

For many years, I doubted whether I was actually connecting to the spirit world and wondered if my 'guides' were just my subconscious mind telling me what I wanted to hear or know. I was reluctant to take my ability seriously and would think, *What if I am just wasting my time and not really achieving anything?* To say I was sceptical is an understatement, but doubt didn't stop the messages from coming. Unless I was convinced the information was truly from spirit, how could I trust or be guided by it? But then, to reject messages that were from a wise and loving source would be just as foolish as blindly accepting my own thoughts as higher guidance.

Meditation is an awareness tool. It can help us to still and know our minds, so that we are better able to distinguish between the thoughts and impulses that are coming from ourselves and the messages or inspiration that might drift in from an external source. At least, that is what I had read. Meditation never really came easy to me as it was something I was not used to. The only form I knew was from self-help books and audios of guided meditations. When endeavouring to meditate without the convenience of a guided meditation, I would close my eyes and see nothing … nothing but darkness. Then I would start wondering how much longer I would have to sit there for. If I couldn't even meditate, how could I be connecting to my guides and how could I make any spiritual progress?

I wanted evidence that the information I was receiving was from outside of myself so, I asked my guides to prove themselves. I also wanted to know I had the ability to meditate and that my efforts were not just a waste of time. I was prepared to give my guides and meditation the opportunity to provide the proof I was looking for, once and for all. So, I enrolled in a course at The Arthur Findlay College in the UK.

My first course was with talented medium, Paul Jacobs. For the whole week, we met every morning before class and meditated for thirty minutes. At Paul's meditation session, he would sit at the front of the room and watch to ensure we sat in stillness with no movement and in total silence. We were led to believe that non-attendance would not reflect well on us, so each day I would dutifully attend.

The first day was the hardest of all. I really didn't know what I was supposed to do while sitting in silence with just my thoughts, but I just went with it wondering how long I had been sitting there and how much longer I would have to be tortured! I was worried I'd nod off to sleep and not truly relax. But as the week went on, I became more comfortable and actually grew to enjoy time out from the world.

Validation of Meditation

Later that same year, at Paul's recommendation, I went back to The Arthur Findlay College to attend his advanced course. This time I was blessed to have Dr Brian Robertson as my tutor. Brian is from Canada and a lovely, gentle soul. The other students talked about his amazing healing powers, so I looked forward to having him as a tutor. In one of his classes he took us through a meditation that led us down a misty path to settle on a bench in a park. When the mist cleared, you would be able to see a loved one from the spirit world sitting opposite you on that bench. I went into this meditation easily and as the mist cleared, I saw a middle-aged man as real as could be.

"Who are you?" I asked. I probably should have said hello first!

"I am your grandfather, William," he replied.

I didn't know him, but I thought he looked a little like my biological dad, and at that stage I had only seen one photo of him. I was well over forty years of age but had never seen a photo of my grandfather—and didn't know how I would get one—but he assured me that he would get a photo to me as proof. He also said I would find out about five events that happened on the same day in the same month. Afterwards, I madly wrote down everything from that meditation in my journal.

The next day, I had a spiritual assessment booked with a tutor called Janet Parker. At a spiritual assessment, they do a reading that discusses your spiritual path. I had not met this tutor before and had told no one of my meditation the day before.

As my assessment started, Janet said, "I know this is supposed to be a spiritual assessment, and not proof of evidence, but I have a man here who says he is your grandfather and that his name is William." I told her I didn't know enough about him to be able to confirm it, to which she replied, "Well, he is saying you have asked for a photo of him and that he is going to ensure you get one. He also tells me he comes from a certain part of England and that you will become aware of five things that happened on the same day in May." I was amazed and shared with her all I'd received in my meditation the day before.

After returning to Hervey Bay, I found a phone number for my grandfather's sister, Aunt Hilda, while cleaning out a drawer in my office. I had received this number many years before, but I had never met her. I kept trying the number, but no one answered, so I took it home and tucked it away safely thinking I would try again one day.

The next morning, a voice in my head told me, "Phone Aunt Hilda." The voice was relentless. It was 6 a.m.—too early—so I called at 9 a.m. It turned out she lived a few streets away from where I worked and had lived there for fifty years. And it was lucky I called. In two weeks, she and her husband were moving to a retirement village, and there was no guarantee they would have the same number. Everything but their essentials were packed up in boxes. She thought she had a photo of my grandfather in there somewhere. She said she'd have a quick look, but I might have to wait for them to unpack at the new address. However, I didn't have to wait until then to finally meet Aunt Hilda. She was so excited to hear from me and I went to see her the very next day.

I was so nervous I took a dear friend with me. I pulled up outside the house and Aunt Hilda, a lovely old lady, greeted me lovingly and said, "Guess what? I found a portrait of your grandfather, William, on top of the first box I opened. Not only that, under it was a copy of our family tree. You and your sister are listed on it."

Aunt Hilda had opened just one of her packing boxes and there on the top was my grandfather's portrait. The man in the photo was the

Validation of Meditation

man from my meditation. During that visit I also came to realise the five things that happened on the same day in the same month.

In the family tree book, I noticed our ancestors had emigrated from the area mentioned in my assessment and had arrived in Australia on 19 May (1). Aunt Hilda told me my father had died on 19 May (2) and that she was unable to attend the funeral as her son had been born that day (3). My parents had been married on 19 May (4), and by coincidence, my husband's parents were also married on that day (5).

Finally, I had proof that I really was connecting during meditation. This information could not possibly have come from my subconscious and it felt as though it was orchestrated by my grandfather from beyond. As a bonus, I also had the blessing of getting to know my great-Aunt Hilda and later, the rest of this beautiful family.

All throughout my spiritual development, I have always asked the spirit world to prove it, to give me evidence, and they always do. I encourage you to do the same.

Now that I have given you proof that meditation really works, I will answer some questions that I am often asked regarding meditation.

What Is Meditation?

Meditation is a practice that focuses on training your awareness, focus and attention. In recent years, research has found that meditating can reduce stress and anxiety, improve focus and concentration, and increase feelings of calm and relaxation.

If you are looking to develop your psychic abilities, the first thing you should do is learn how to breathe and meditate. Just five minutes a day will go a long way. The idea is to quieten your conscious mind (meditation) so that you will be able to receive messages from the spirit side. Once you've quietened your mind the communication channel will begin to open. Without a quiet mind it is like trying to listen to more than one conversation at a time and understand all of them.

When you meditate, connect with the Divine Source. Do this to develop your own power. Your awareness is like a muscle: the more you flex it, the stronger it gets, and the more comfortable you become with it, so practise, practise, practise.

I have noticed that I seem to receive clear information in the shower, or upon waking up. This is because I am more relaxed, and my mind clutter is at a minimum. You can meditate with your eyes open and still see the pictures in your mind or hear the thoughts in your head.

When you're new to meditation it is sometimes hard to know where to start; I know it was like that for me. I would close my eyes and wait for something to happen. Guess what? Not much did! Mostly my meditations were for the purpose of connecting prior to readings, which were short and happened at the beginning of any day I was doing readings. They were really a way of setting my intention, being that I wanted to turn on all my intuitive gifts; that I wanted accuracy; that I wanted to connect to my clients' loved ones in spirit; and, finally, that the client would be happy with the reading.

At college the tutor didn't advise me on how to meditate, as it wasn't a beginners' class and it was assumed that everyone knew what was expected. The tutor told us to come into the class, take a seat and start meditating and he would let us know when thirty minutes had passed by. After a couple of days of this, I worked out my own way and it worked. You could say my spirit team taught me.

Validation of Meditation

I knew that relaxing was important. The teacher advised the class that stillness was a must, so no fidgeting or movement. I was too embarrassed to ask anyone what was expected and how to do it. So, I just sat there, closed my eyes and waited.

The first two days I thought I was being punished! It felt way too long to sit in meditation. I was mainly used to listening to a guided meditation. By the third day I had worked out a routine. By the sixth day I was loving it and promised myself that I would faithfully meditate every day. Ha! That was not how it worked out. Life does get in the way, especially when you have a young family, pets and a busy lifestyle.

My Six-Step Process to Meditate for Connection

Below I have set out in an easy format the steps I would take to meditate with the intention of connecting to the spirit world. I don't want to assume you already have a way of your own. You may like to try it this way.

1. Close your eyes and take three deep breaths, making the exhaled breath longer than the inhaled breath. I decided that those three breaths were the trigger that told my spirit team that I was going to meditate.
2. Then I would ask to connect to my 'guides and helpers from the highest source of all that is good'. I know when I am connected as I feel an energy change, a 'shift'. Sometimes my students don't feel that change and then it comes down to trusting that they are connected.
3. Then I would ask for guidance or assistance. Sometimes I would ask a question, or I would think about what I wanted to know about. As you learnt above, initially I thought it was all in my mind.

4. From that point the conversation would flow; sometimes it took time, it depended on me and how relaxed and ready I was.
5. I can also feel an energy change when the connection has stopped.
6. Once I feel the energy connection has gone, I take a deep breath and slowly open my eyes.

When you have finished you might like to write down in your psychic journal the details from your meditation. As the information is channelled, it can be like a dream, and quickly you forget about it if you don't write it down.

Is Meditation Beneficial?

Meditation can assist with the development of spiritual awareness. It has been known to lower blood pressure and have positive health benefits. It can also bring peace and calmness into a chaotic lifestyle. It is a form of escape from the trials and tribulations of everyday life.

Why Is It Important to Meditate?

Meditation is the foundation of everything you do when developing your intuitive gifts. It can discipline your mind to hold a spiritual 'contact' for long periods. It assists in training your mind to be still enough to connect to the spirit world without the distractions of the material world. We meditate to develop clarity, intuition and guidance.

Validation of Meditation

How Often Should You Meditate?

Ideally, take time to be still in silence every day, preferably at the same time for a minimum of 30 minutes, if you can. By meditating at the same time every day, you are making an appointment and saying that you are available for communication. This also shows commitment to the spirit world.

Once you are disciplined it will just be a matter of saying "I am ready to work." You will develop so much quicker if you meditate.

It is okay if you don't meditate every day, as it is not always convenient to do so. Five minutes whenever you can is better than not meditating at all.

Don't worry about time when you are meditating. If you start to feel a little antsy, and you find yourself constantly thinking about how long you have been meditating, or whether you have been in meditation long enough, you might as well stop, as you are no longer focused. If you only have a limited amount of time, then it is a good idea to set a timer that gently alerts you to when you need to stop.

What Are Some of the Different Forms of Meditation Used by the Developing Psychic?

I have listed different types of meditations below and by no means are they the only ones available.

- Intention meditation—used to set an intention for what you want to achieve, e.g. to program a crystal, or for a particular subject
- Connection meditation—for the purpose of connecting to a higher power

- Re-programming meditation—to change the way you think, act, believe and to break patterns
- Guided meditation—you are guided by someone else's voice and normally for a purpose, e.g. relaxation, healing, past life connection, etc.
- Chanting meditation—focusing on your breath while you repeat a word, e.g. "Om"
- Walking meditation—walking and focusing on only what you can see; helps to increase your focus and awareness
- Visual meditation—focusing on something serene and peaceful, may even be a recording of peaceful scenes
- Healing meditation—for the purpose of healing
- Relaxation meditation—for peace, calm and relaxation
- Focused meditation—you focus on an object, e.g. a candle flame or a crystal, or mala beads
- Mindfulness meditation—you pay attention to your thoughts as they pass through your mind
- Trance meditation—used to go into a trance state
- Creative meditation—used for visualising goals

Does It Matter If I Fall Asleep?

If you meditate in a subdued light you could fall asleep. If you do fall asleep the spirit world can still work with the energy, you are just not aware of it. It is like falling asleep in a meeting; you are not aware of anything, but the meeting is still happening.

Are Guided Meditations a Better Option?

With guided meditations you are listening to the meditation and following the instructions, and usually for a purpose. When you do

Validation of Meditation

a silent meditation, you can have the intention of opening up to listen to spirit and receive their messages. Silence allows you to use all your senses without distraction. Sometimes your environment may not facilitate complete silence. This is not an issue as background noise will fade the deeper you go into the meditation.

When you find the stillness and quietness, an hour can feel like 10 minutes; there is no awareness of time.

There are many ways and reasons to meditate. It is up to you to decide what type of meditation you favour and how long you meditate for. If you are new to meditation, I suggest you start with short meditations. You will eventually find what works for you.

Psychic Protection

Don't let their negative energy drain you
— Scottie Waves.

"I feel like I am having a heart attack," I said as I woke up, clutching my chest; the pain took my breath away.

This was the third morning in a row that I had awoken to a sharp pain in my chest that didn't last for very long.

"Do you want me to call an ambulance?" Tony asked with a concerned look, and I could see he was trying not to panic.

We were staying in a unit at the coast and this was the same conversation we had had every morning since we arrived. It was beginning to feel like *Groundhog Day*. I wouldn't let him call an ambulance. The thought came into my head that something had happened in this room and I was picking up the energy. Once the pain went, I was right for the day. That is one of the downsides of being an empath (clairsentient); it is quite common for me to pick up the energy around me and take on the feelings of others.

"I think it is something to do with this bed," I exclaimed.

"What if we turn the mattress over or I sleep on that side, will that fix it?" Tony asked.

"No, I don't think that will do it; I am not sure what it is, or why it is happening," I said vaguely.

Later in the day I was explaining to my daughter Chloe what had been happening.

"Mum, did you remember to protect the bed, like you taught me?" Chloe asked.

"Oh no, I didn't! Such a 'rookie' mistake," I replied.

I hadn't protected the bed or the unit when we arrived, as we had quickly rushed out to an appointment. I had not even thought to do it and now I was paying the price.

I quickly projected my protection symbol onto the bed and then did a clearing and protected the whole unit. The next morning the energy was gone, the heart attack feeling was gone.

At the end of our stay I went to reception to check out and return the key.

Psychic Protection

"Do you know if anyone had a heart attack in the unit we stayed in?" I asked the receptionist, who was the lady that managed all the units, so I figured she would know if anyone did. Her eyes went wide and her mouth dropped.

"Did you know her?" she questioned. "We were trying to keep it a secret as nobody will want to stay in that unit if they find out that someone recently died there."

"No, I was just wondering," I replied.

"How did you find out about it?" she questioned, looking very puzzled as she knew I was a tourist and not from this area. I dodged her question and asked another one of my own.

"Did it happen in the early hours of the morning?"

"Yes," she replied. I then quickly changed the subject, thanked her and left quickly. I am sure she probably thought I was some sort of weirdo.

It was good to confirm my insight and I had more evidence of proof that psychic protection is not only important, it also really, really works. If only I would remember to use it more often. This experience also confirmed that clearing energy works too.

When the spirit world wants to get through to me they will find a way. Some are curious, others just want to let me know that they are there. It is not unusual for me to feel their energy.

Tony and I travel a lot and if the hotel we are staying in is 'haunted' then the spirits will find me. Tony finds it annoying and it happens a lot. Those stories will be in my next book … *The Modern Oracle, My Crazy Psychic Life;* that is what I am calling the book at this stage.

I didn't always use psychic protection; there was a time when I hadn't even heard of it, let alone know what it was, and I know I am not on my own with this. As your psychic gifts develop further and become stronger, you will find that it will be beneficial for you to protect your energy.

Years ago, when I used to teach students one on one, I had a student who had just begun training with me. During her first lesson I announced that I was going to teach her about psychic protection.

"Do you protect yourself?" I asked.

She looked at me and paused as she thought about it, before replying, "I always ask my partners to wear condoms."

My jaw started to drop as I looked at her, and I thought, *Surely she is joking*, but as I looked at her face, I realised she was serious. I had to keep a straight face and not laugh as I didn't want to appear rude.

"That's really good and I'm happy to hear that, but you also need to protect your energy. I have a little exercise to protect your psychic energy," I replied.

"What am I protecting it from?" she asked.

"From your energy being drained or affected. When you're clairsentient you can be vulnerable," I answered. I then went on to teach her the exercises I have added to this chapter.

Psychic Protection

Do you ever feel like you have a sign on your forehead that says, "Tell me your problems?" Even people you have never met before, or don't know really well, sometimes feel compelled to tell you their problems. That happens a lot when you are a healer, as people are drawn unconsciously to your energy. Once they have dumped all their issues onto you, they feel better. As an empath sometimes you become a magnet for those people who are hurting. All this energy then stays in your aura unless you clear it away.

It is okay to listen, and most often it is therapeutic for the person, but don't take it on board and make it part of your life. These people can drain your energy. Most of the time they are expelling negative energy, and they can be commonly referred to as 'psychic vampires'.

Psychic Vampires (Energy Drainers)

So, what is a psychic vampire?

They are people who drain your energy, they feed off your energy. Sometimes you are not even aware of it until it has happened. You know when you have been around these people, as they make you feel drained, be it when you are with them or even just talking to them on the phone. They're the ones that when you recognise their number, you don't want to answer the phone, especially if you don't have a spare hour to listen to all their issues.

The psychic vampire can have a negative energy; this does not mean that they are bad people, they just deal with life in a different way. We can all have negative energy at certain times. Times when we feel down or upset. But these people are like this 24/7, they just go from one drama to the next and they enjoy reliving them. Most of the time they do not realise that they are pulling your energy down as they dump their issues on you. They then feel better and energised afterwards. When they have their next drama, they will enjoy telling you again, because it makes them feel better, but it can leave you feeling drained or depressed. These people make you want to avoid them but sometimes it is not possible. Listen to what they have to say, if you feel you must. Some people we can't escape as we may be related to them, or there is no nice way to do it. During these times you need to activate psychic protection and put a barrier around you, something that will bounce that negative energy off of you.

Positive energy dissolves negative energy; like attracts like. Be positive to attract positive people and energy.

Psychic Attack

People who drain our energy field and leave you feeling exhausted are using a form of psychic attack. Most of the time they are not even aware that they are doing it. Holding in anger and resentment towards others is another form of psychic attack which lowers your and their energy.

Sceptics Are Energy Drainers

Most people fear what they can't understand or control. There will always be sceptics, detractors and energy drainers. Let's face it, everyone can be wrong at some time. We just expect psychics to be accurate 100% of the time, or people will say that they are not a good psychic. Not even doctors are 100% right and most of us remember that dodgy haircut we received from someone that came highly recommended. Even the best psychics make mistakes, as it all comes down to the interpretation of the message they are receiving. They are only human! They can be affected

Psychic Protection

by their surroundings and emotions. Most sceptics don't understand how it all works. So, they will drain your energy, take away your power with their words and actions if you let them. Do not give their words energy. Everyone is entitled to their opinions and beliefs. Even all the religions cannot agree on all the same beliefs. Sceptics are entitled to their way of thinking. Let them get on with it and with their life. You do not have to prove yourself. What you do is not a party trick. We are here to bring about an awareness of the spiritual life.

"Watch out for the magpie, it is coming right for you!" Tony yelled out as we walked along the street.

I looked over at him and saw that he was dodging and darting to get away from the birds as they swooped, aiming for his head.

"We will be fine, don't worry about it," I replied.

"That is easy for you to say, you're not the one being attacked. How come they are leaving you alone?"

"I put a bubble of white light protection around me," I replied. He looked at me with disbelief as if I was crazy.

"Well why didn't you put one around me?" he angrily retorted.

"It was already around me from when I protected myself this morning. I will put one around you now," I replied. I beamed the protection around him and the birds went away.

I knew the way my husband thought, and this was just a bit far-fetched for him to believe in. By now his brain was turning what had happened into a coincidence, and the reason the birds stopped swooping was that we had moved further away, even though they didn't attack me.

Psychic protection is simple, it's easy and shouldn't take too long to do.

There are many books available on psychic protection and some of them are more than a couple inches thick. I like to teach psychic protection in a simple way. Of course, if you don't believe it works, it most likely won't. My way of teaching is to simplify the way things are done if possible.

There are many times where I may have forgotten to protect myself and I quickly have to do a clearing, and then protect myself. The following exercises will be beneficial for you regarding protection and clearing energy.

Protection Exercise

Close your eyes.

Relax and take three deep, cleansing breaths in and out.

Visualise the white or gold light (whichever you prefer working with) entering through the top of your head (crown chakra), and as you are doing this say the following (does not have to be out loud).

"I bring in the white light" *(visualise the white light entering through your crown chakra and travelling down through your whole body)*.

"I radiate the white light" *(visualise the white light radiating out of your body)*.

Psychic Protection

"**I am the white light.**"

"**I now put the golden sphere of protection around me**" *(visualise this).*

"**I now surround myself with a protective, reflective, mirrored bubble that reflects all negativity and attracts positively, love and light**" *(visualise this).*

"**I am grounded**" *(visualise roots coming out of your feet and travelling down deep into the earth).*

Clearing Exercise

The clearing exercise is used to clear your energy (aura).

We go through the day picking up energy from other people. Although we should protect ourselves psychically, sometimes we just forget. We can also be vulnerable when we open ourselves to read for people and connect to the spirit world as a medium.

By the end of the day your aura can contain lots of different energies, especially if you are clairsentient, an empath.

This exercise is good to do throughout your day (depending on the different energies you may encounter) and especially at the end of the day before crawling into bed.

This exercise is about letting go and releasing.

Close your eyes.
Relax and take three deep, cleansing breaths in and out.
Ask God or the Universe to clear you.

"Please clear my mind, body and soul."
"Clear my mind, body and soul."
"Please clear me psychically."
"Clear me psychically."
"Amen and so it is."

Now visualise any attachments or chords that you may have picked up during the day dissolving. In your mind visualise your body covered with a 'dissolving foam' that dissolves any attachments. Then rinse off with cleansing white light.

Intention

Our intention creates our reality
—Wayne Dyer.

"Katy, will you please do a reading and look into my spiritual path? It will give you some practice as well," Anne asked.

When Anne made this request, I was in the very early days of my development and I still had my corporate career. I hadn't even had any formal training as it was before I attended the Arthur Findlay College, and many other spiritual workshops and courses that were to come. At that time, to grow my confidence, I would practise on willing friends and colleagues in my spare time.

Anne was a delightful lady, with the energy of a wise sage. We had worked together for a few months and she was very much spiritually minded. When Anne was with me, she would often question me about different things, and the information that I would channel would answer her questions as well as enlighten me at the same time. Thinking back, I do believe that Anne came into my life for the purpose of helping me develop further. My time with Anne was a catalyst for change, a turning point for me.

Reluctantly I started her reading, and as more information came out, that she could confirm, the more confidence I was gaining. As the reading progressed, she became happier and happier with the reading.

"I don't know why intention kept coming up," she said.

"I do! It is because you have not been using it lately; you may know all about intention, but you've lost the practice of using it. You need to reconnect, and work with the power of intention," I replied.

"Yes, I stopped when I ceased reading for others. I always felt connected to spirit when I was doing readings. I have since gotten out of the habit of setting the intention to connect. I now realise that I left behind a lot of my practices," she confirmed.

A lot more information came up in her reading, and I could feel her energy getting lighter as I continued. She was making a list as I spoke. One of the things on the list was to work with a spiritual 'tool', one that she felt she connected with. I then heard the word 'colour' in my head.

"Anne, have you ever thought of working with colour?" I said.

Her face brightened and she replied, "I have just started getting back into colour, another practice that I had left behind."

Intention

"See, you are already on your way," I stated. By the time the reading had finished she was feeling re-energised.

After the reading I made it my mission to find out as much as I could about intention and then discovered the book *The Power of Intention* by Dr. Wayne Dyer.

To further develop your intuitive gifts, you need to set an intention.

Intention is the starting point of every dream, desire or goal. It is the creative power that fulfils all of our needs, whether for a spiritual awakening or further development.

What Is Intention?

Intention is defined as 'a thing intended; an aim or plan: a determination or plan to do a specific thing'. An example of intention is someone going to art school.

The power of intention is the power of a focused mind. When focusing our mental energy on something, we're able to give more of our brain power to it.

Setting Your Spiritual Intention

To set your spiritual intention you first have to know what you want; e.g. *I want to develop my psychic powers*. Then plant the seed in your mind, so that it can start to grow in the direction you desire. When you focus your mental energy on your desire and give it more of your brain power, you put your mind in the right position to perform at a maximum level to enable you to achieve your goal. Once you have done that you will now start to notice opportunities to achieve your goal. Opportunities that you may not have noticed before you set your intention. From there you need to continually focus on what you are trying to achieve and allow it to happen.

To empower your intention, it is also good to visualise yourself achieving your intention and think about what it would look like. What you could do once you achieve your intention. For example, if your intention was to develop your psychic powers, what would it look like once you were more psychic, how would it affect your life?

I now believe that the power of intention is the power behind developing your spiritual gifts.

If you intend to connect to the spirit world, you will, as long as you also trust that you can. You need to believe in this power for it to happen; e.g. if you intend to write a book, then with motivation and knowledge you will write a book.

One example of working with intention that I often witness is the confusion that my students have about whether to work with the white light or gold light for energy protection. My answer is that it is determined by what you believe. My belief is that the white light is for protection and the gold light is for manifesting. Many others believe it is the other way around or even something different. I feel that it is a personal preference, and you should go with what feels right for you. It can also come down to what you believe or who you have been influenced by.

A lot of psychics have routines that they go through before they do psychic readings. Some of the routines are really elaborate and others are just a matter of saying a prayer for what you want (setting the intention), and then doing the readings. I even know a psychic who

Intention

says, "I am connected to the highest source, and so it is." All of them believe that the way they connect is the right way for them. A good way to confirm your beliefs is to write them down. I encourage my students to start their 'dictionary' of meanings. This can be at the back of their psychic diary/journal or a separate book. This is where you write down the meanings of symbols, or signs that the spirit world communicate to you, e.g. what a butterfly means to you or if the spirit world shows you roses then they are communicating this to you. Everyone is different and has different ways of communicating. There are also many different ways that the spirit world can work and communicate with you, and they may not be the same way that others do.

It is good to learn how spirit communicates with you. Think of it as if you're starting a new language and compiling a dictionary. That dictionary can be full of symbols, and the symbols can come from experience.

A well-known symbol is the heart shape. Most of us think of love when we see a heart. You would write in your diary, heart = love.

A butterfly can have several meanings. When I am asked what I think a butterfly means, I answer "freedom". Why? Because generally when I see a butterfly it is very free, flittering around the flowers. The butterfly does not have the knowledge that it doesn't have a long life span. It doesn't have bills to pay or the worries that people have. Another known meaning for the butterfly is 'transition', as in transition from one state to another, e.g. death, going from a physical form to a spiritual form upon dying. The butterfly can also be interpreted as 'fragile', i.e. the butterfly's wings are known to be fragile and easily damaged.

That is three meanings for a butterfly that I have mentioned. It would be up to you to decide what a butterfly symbolises and then write it down in your psychic journal to confirm the meaning, e.g. when you show me a butterfly it means this. Choosing all three meanings can leave you feeling confused as to which one to use.

You would have to think to yourself, *Which meaning do I relate to the most?* Then you would set the intention with the spirit world that when they show you a butterfly it means freedom or transition, or fragile. This is your language that you are creating and your dictionary.

Another time, I was with a friend who had just bought a particular crystal for a purpose.

She bought the crystal to help keep her weight down. Managing weight was not one of the believed properties of this crystal; it was, though, just the right shape and colour for her. She then set the intention with this crystal and programmed it. The intention was that whenever she would hold the crystal it would suppress her appetite and remind her to only eat healthy foods. Did it work? Yes, because she believed in the intention she set.

Exercise: Programming a Crystal With 'Intention'

Why program a crystal?

The purpose of programming a crystal is to focus its energies on a specific goal, intention or desire. A programmed crystal becomes more powerful, useful and effective. You charge the crystal with your intention. Your intention should follow the natural properties of the crystal to harness their energy, e.g. use a channelling crystal for the purpose of channelling.

How do I program a crystal?

Intention

You can program a crystal for a particular purpose with the power of 'intention' by using the following steps.

1. Cleanse your crystal

You can do this by using one of the following methods; not all methods are listed. Research your crystal first to check which methods are better for your crystal as not all methods are good for all crystals; there are some crystals that should not be cleansed in water.

- Intention—ask for it to be cleared
- Hold your crystal under running water
- Wash your crystal in the ocean. Be careful not to lose your crystal
- Bury your crystal in the earth (remember to mark where you buried it so you can find it again)
- Smudge it with a sacred herb, e.g. sage
- Reiki can clear and program a crystal
- Place your crystal out in the moonlight, full moon is optimum
- Cover them with brown rice
- Sound cleansing (sound vibration) with crystal singing bowls, Tibetan bowls, tuning forks, etc.

2. Activate your crystal

First determine why you are wanting to program your crystal and what its intended purpose is, e.g. for healing, for protection, to channel with, to improve your focus or even to assist you to break a habit. It is up to you to decide and set the intention.

First cleanse your crystal.
Then hold your crystal in your hands and focus on it.
Imagine that you are connected to this crystal by an invisible cord of energy and then say out loud:
"I invite my guides and helpers to dedicate this crystal for the highest good of all who come in contact with it, and for the purpose of ………… (fill in your purpose here). Amen and so it is."

Proof of Connection: Cooking With Yaya

What is now proved, was once only imagination
—William Blake.

Have you ever wondered if some of the thoughts that pop into your head could be from a loved one in the spirit world, or maybe even your guides?

Many students are confused about whether they are channelling, connecting to the spirit world or if it is just all in their mind. They write it off as their imagination. I must admit, I too was confused and doubtful. I thought I was telling myself what I wanted to hear. When I thought that my dad was saying he loved me, it was quickly followed by the thought, *Of course he would say that*, as that is what I would expect to hear; therefore, *It is all in my imagination*. Messages can also be your ego talking (what you want to hear) or based on a fear.

How do you tell the difference? Well, the experience for each person can differ. I know when I am connected to the spirit world, whether it is channelling or mediumship, the messages come through very quickly and if I don't say them, or write them down, they disappear just as quick.

Just like when you have a dream and forget the details; if you don't discuss it or write the details down the dreams fade.

I am known for talking faster when I am doing readings and will write down what I am receiving at the same time as I am talking, in case I miss passing on a message. There can be many forms of distractions that cause an interruption to the flow of energy, including the client speaking, which I don't mind. Then I will refer back to the piece of paper to see what I am yet to mention. It took me a while to fine tune this skill and the more readings I did, the stronger and more confident I became.

Over the years I have had many connections with my family in spirit. A lot of the time when I am receiving messages, I don't even realise it. I don't try to work out who is talking to me, as when I do that my brain is getting in the way and I feel like the stream of messages stops flowing. Most of the time I have not met the relative in spirit, so I don't identify them easily. All my grandparents and beyond them were dead before I was born except for my father's mother who wanted nothing to do with my sister and I. So, the only information I had was via stories and anecdotes that my mother would sometimes tell about her family.

Proof of Connection: Cooking With Yaya

The first recollection I have of knowingly conversing with one of my ancestors was with my great-grandmother, my mother's grandmother (Yaya) who raised Mum and her siblings from a very young age. At the time it felt like I was having an argument with myself in my head. I wanted to do one thing and my great-grandmother had definite ideas about what she wanted me to do.

I am telling you this story so you can get an idea of the subtle ways, or, in the case of my great-grandmother, not-so-subtle ways, that our loved ones in spirit can connect.

One day on my way home from the gym, I felt the urge to stop off at a grocery store to pick up a couple of items for lunch.

In my head, thoughts started to come in prompting me to buy other ingredients, but I didn't know in what way I would be using them. When I had to buy a tin of crushed tomatoes, I remember thinking about how much I hated any sort of tomato unless it was blended down to nothing, like tomato sauce or paste, because I found tomatoes bitter in taste. She requested that I buy raw chicken as well as other ingredients too, and as I felt so compelled, I just went with it. I didn't end up buying the raw chicken as I already had some chicken breast fillets at home. I had learnt by this stage of my life to trust whatever the voice in my head was saying. I thought, *What I am going to do with all those ingredients?*

We are making soup, was the thought that rapidly popped into my head.

When I arrived home, I unpacked the groceries and prepared to sit down and watch a music show that I enjoyed. As I headed towards the TV, I had the following thought: *We are making soup, get the big saucepan out.* I remember thinking that I didn't want to make soup. Then the thought was repeated and along with it was the compelling urge to listen to it.

I set off into the kitchen to look for a big saucepan. *Bigger than that* was the next thought, which I will now refer to as a voice. I looked until I found the biggest saucepan I had. From that point I followed her instructions. When it came to add the chicken, she didn't seem impressed with my choice of chicken breast that I was busy chopping. She wanted to use a chicken frame (the bones) and I assumed that this was to make the stock. I didn't have a chicken frame and it was easier to buy ready-made chicken stock.

This spirit appeared to be very direct and no-nonsense, loving but firm and not to be messed with. She said she was my great-grandmother. Images were popping into my head as she kept talking and she showed me, in my mind, little pictures of what she wanted me to do. I proceeded to follow her orders and thought *This soup is going to be yuck!* It contained ingredients that I would not normally eat. *Oh well, Tony will eat it, he'll try anything,* I thought, as I continued to follow her instructions.

I rang my mother and asked her if her grandmother used to make soup out of these ingredients. She said, "Yes." Mum went on to confirm my great-grandmother's personality, and that I was definitely communicating with her. After I hung up the phone my great-grandmother said that the soup was for cleansing the kidneys and I was to take it over to my uncle's place for him to eat. So, I rang my mother again and asked if her grandmother thought that the soup was for cleansing the kidneys and she said, "Yes." Then my great-grandmother wanted me to add basil. As I went to reach for the dried herbs, she firmly told me, *Not those, the fresh basil in the garden, why do you think I got you to plant it?* Now I knew that I didn't want to eat this soup with the fresh basil in it. I am somewhat finicky but getting better as I get older. She told me I would love it and it would be good for me. I kept going until the voice stopped. When it went quiet, I thought, *I must be finished.*

Proof of Connection: Cooking With Yaya

Tony came into the kitchen and asked what I was cooking. Without thinking, I replied, "I am making soup to take to Uncle George to heal his kidneys."

"What is wrong with his kidneys and does he know that we are coming to visit?" he asked.

"No, I am going to call him now," I answered, and I bypassed the kidney question as I didn't have an answer. Up until Tony asked me what I was doing I didn't even know that there was a purpose for making the soup. It was a surprise to me as well as to Tony. I made the call and we headed over to their house with the soup and a loaf of crusty bread.

We were all sitting around the table and my Uncle George asked, "What do you call this soup, it tastes exactly like the soup my grandmother used to make for us and she always used to say that it was good for our kidneys."

As I explained the soup-making process and ingredients, he mentioned that the only difference was that his grandmother always used a chicken frame, not a chicken breast, as that was how it was done way back then. I wasn't sure if the soup would actually cleanse the kidneys, but it was my great-grandmother's belief and that is how she got her message through. We had a lovely family lunch and it was accepted well. Yes, I did eat the soup and it was delicious.

A month later I drove my Uncle George and Aunty Joy to Brisbane to see their financial planner. While we were there, I felt compelled to talk them into visiting a Chinese herbalist that I had great faith in. I just had this urge that they should visit him. The Chinese herbalist announced that my uncle had a problem with his kidneys, confirming Yaya's message. Uncle George could not accept this but played along with it to humour me. A couple of weeks later Uncle George was in immense pain and was found to have kidney stones. If only he had listened to his grandmother!

Our minds require experiences and proof for us to believe the unbelievable. A lot of people will not put their trust in anything until they see it with their own eyes, until they witness or prove the inconceivable. I, too, am sceptical until I have proof or witness the experience. I always say to my spirit team, "If this is so, then prove it." I ask this about anything that I think might just be my imagination or a desire. Obviously, the above story was proven twice over and that enabled me to be more confident in my gifts. With proof comes trust, with trust comes confidence.

Do you ever hear a voice in your head that sounds different to the way you think? Don't discount it, as it might just be someone trying to communicate with you. How will you know? A lot of the time it can be random thoughts that pop into your head. Sometimes the spirit world communicates via music. A song comes into your head that you know you haven't heard for a while. It may well be the words of the song are important or the song was a favourite of a loved one in spirit. Images may form in your head, or you get a particular feeling when they are communicating with you.

Those in spirit can also communicate in many other ways, e.g. through electronics. My sister Julianne once discovered our deceased dad's computer turned on with a family photo on the screen that was not the screensaver. That computer had been turned off for weeks; no one had been using it. Julianne was delighted to see that particular photo as it carried a message for her.

My car windscreen wipers continued to move backwards and forwards after I took the key out. I ran into the office and asked my PA Brie to

Proof of Connection: Cooking With Yaya

check it out. Lights flickering is a common one when I am around. My husband was a bit freaked out to find a light on in a room that neither of us turned on. I could feel the spirit energy and the light was proof.

I have had books jump off a bookshelf and land near my feet, open at a pertinent page. If the spirit world wants to get a message to you, they will find a way. Let's hope you are paying attention to notice it. In the above story I was using my claircognizance (clear knowing), my clairvoyance (clear seeing) and my clairaudience (clear hearing). It was automatically changing throughout the contact.

Finally, let's talk about how to determine the source of the information and if it is actually a connection, as it can also be a fear that you have, your ego wanting it to happen or a prophetic vision. I will explain these further.

Prophecy is a vision that comes out of nowhere, positive or negative. It has no emotion attached to it. A message comes quickly and then it is gone. This is a message from your spirit team.

Fears or desires are when you receive a message and simultaneously emotions are involved. You are more than likely picking up on your fears or desires. Therefore, not a message from your spirit team.

Ego is mainly experienced through your desire to experience a vision or a desire to impress someone with your gift. Your mind will be racing with thoughts and there will be mixed feelings of excitement and fear. Therefore, not a message from your spirit team.

When your mind fabricates a vision or message, the images go on and on and seem to get more elaborate with time and it is likely that emotions will be attached. How do you sort this out and discern what type of message you are getting? You ask your intuition for the truth.

The following is a two-part exercise to help you distinguish what you are receiving by answering the questions after each part, e.g. prophetic vision, fear or ego.

Exercise:

If I was to ask you to close your eyes for a minute and see if a message comes through, there is a high chance that you will either receive nothing or continue to think your normal thoughts. Give it a try now. Now write down the results in your journal.

Now if I was to ask you to connect first as per the following exercise, you will have a better chance of receiving a message. The more you do the exercise the better you will get. If you repeat it often it will get easier and the connection will grow stronger.

Connection exercise:

1. Find a quiet place to sit and totally relax your body.
2. Set the intention that you want a message of guidance.
3. Close your eyes and take three long, deep breaths and exhale each breath slowly.
4. Do your clearing exercise to clear any information that may be on your mind or any fears and doubts you are currently feeling; this will help you to break any thought patterns.
5. Continue the deep breaths for about a minute or so.
6. Now visualise that there is a continuous white light beaming down from the Universe and connecting to the crown of your head (crown chakra) and then flowing down through your body and totally surrounding you.
7. Ask for a message of guidance as you continue to meditate.

Proof of Connection: Cooking With Yaya

8. Be open to anything you receive. This message could come in the form of a symbol, colour, picture, you might even hear the message in your mind.
9. Keep meditating until you either feel a disconnection or stop receiving anything. Some of you will notice a change in energy.
10. When you are finished open your eyes.

Now write about your experience and answer the following questions in your psychic journal.

- *Did you find it hard or easy to connect?*
- *How did you receive the information (prophecy, fear, desire or ego)?*
- *Did the message come out of nowhere or was it prompted by something you recently witnessed or heard, e.g. a song you recently heard?*
- *Was there emotion attached?*

After you finish this exercise, I hope you will be able to distinguish the type of message you are receiving and where or who it is coming from. With practice you will get better.

Eventually you won't even need to go through the above steps. You will just 'connect' and start a conversation. As I proved in the above story. The spirit world can also pay you an impromptu visit, when needed. Just like my Yaya did.

Messages From Beyond: Proof of Life After Death

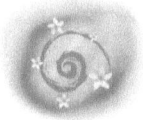

The spirit world is sending you messages through signs in your everyday life. Listen closely to them, nothing is a coincidence

—Matt Fraser.

Dad was dying! My stepdad, Barry, was the only dad I ever knew, and I called him 'Dad'.

He was a sceptic and didn't believe in anything spiritual. He had been in hospital for a long time and wasn't expected to see the end of the year.

The Modern Oracle

I had a trip booked to attend the Arthur Findlay College in England and I was hesitant about going. What if he died when I was so far away? I took a deep breath and intuitively felt it would be fine to go; I needed to trust my intuition.

The week at college went well and I was chosen to represent our class demonstrating mediumship in the Sanctuary, for the local service. During the demonstration I was expected to make a link to someone in spirit in front of a packed church and deliver their message. To say I was nervous was an understatement. Anxiety was setting in and then to compound it, I received a message that Dad would be having brain surgery at approximately the same time. I wasn't sure that I was going to be able to perform in my stressed state.

I decided to go for a walk in the beautiful college gardens to calm myself down and make my decision. I knew my tutor would be disappointed in me if I didn't participate and he also didn't know about my dad. I didn't want to be seen to be making excuses to get out of doing the demonstration. As I was walking and contemplating, the guidance I received was to 'go ahead with the performance'. It would prove that I would be able to still make a connection while under stress. I also had the song 'I Have a Dream' by Abba on repeat in my head, as I had heard it earlier in the week at the college church service. This song would end up being one of Dad's calling cards when he was communicating with us.

An hour later, I was sitting in a chair, on the church platform, looking out at the audience. The other students that had been selected from other classes were just as nervous.

When it was my turn, I stood up and connected to a young lad who had died in a motorbike accident recently. I delivered his message to his mother who was in the congregation, as she sat there quietly sobbing. The time went quickly, and it was not long before I was back sitting in my seat. I had done it and I was amazed that I could, under so much pressure.

When I arrived back from my overseas trip, my brother Michael was waiting at the airport to take me to visit Dad in the few hours before my next flight home. While I was visiting, I played the following songs on my iPad: 'I Have a Dream' by Abba and 'A Hundred Thousand Angels' by Bliss. Mum and Dad both enjoyed the songs. I had rediscovered those two songs while at college.

On my next visit to see my parents, Dad's mother, Jessie, appeared before me in the hospital room, with a message that she was taking her 'boy' in two weeks' time. This proved to be true.

"Dad, I know you don't believe in the afterlife, but if you find out you were wrong, could you send us a sign?" I asked. "What sign would you like to send us?" I added. He looked over at the poster on the wall that his grandchildren had made for him and pointed to it. There was a little plastic yellow butterfly on the poster, and he wanted it. I retrieved it from the poster and handed it to him. He then stuck the butterfly on the left side of his hospital gown. "So, Dad, you will show a butterfly as a sign?" I asked, and he nodded his head.

Chloe then said, "I want you to show me a feather, Grandad." Dad nodded his head and smiled at her.

Days later Dad was lying in his hospital bed, non-responsive, and he was not waking up! Mum had requested that I give him a Reiki healing. The doctors had announced that Dad was not going to be with us for much longer. His room was full of family members around his bed and then someone decided we should sing all his favourite songs to him and see if that would wake him up. You could feel the love in the air. After about an hour of singing, we were all flagging and now repeating songs, when Dad suddenly opened his eyes and looked around the room. Dad was back!

The family continued to do the designated shifts that were 24/7 so that someone was always with Mum and Dad as our mother was refusing to leave Dad's side. Tony had announced that he was taking the kids home so that they didn't miss any more school and they were flying home tomorrow. I didn't get much sleep that night, I was very restless, and I had an uneasy feeling; the energy felt different. When I wasn't asleep, I was staring at the ceiling with the song 'I Have a Dream' playing on repeat in my head. I kept seeing Dad pushing his head through a veil of water, peering down at me. Early morning, I got up and got dressed.

Tony asked, "What are you doing? It is too early, go back to sleep."

"I'm getting dressed because Michael is going to call to tell me that Katie is having the baby, and he wants me to cover his shift."

Tony replied, "But the baby is not due yet."

I looked at him and said, "Yeah, I know that. It is just what I feel." Only minutes later, Michael called to repeat what I had just mentioned to Tony, that they were having their baby, and he wanted his shift covered.

"Tony, do you have to go home today? I feel that Dad is going to die today," I said.

"Everyone has been thinking that for days, and the kids really need to get back to school," he replied.

Messages From Beyond: Proof of Life After Death

Michael called to announce the arrival of a healthy baby boy and asked me to put him on speaker to tell Dad. When the call ended, Mum asked my sister Julianne and I to go to the other hospital and visit with Michael and Katie to spread the love and congratulate them on baby Lachlan's birth. "I don't want to leave you right now, Mum, I am not going, Julianne can go, and I will stay here with you."

Mum then angrily told us to go. Reluctantly, Julianne and I left with me cradling her baby Beni. No sooner had we got out of the lift than I said, "Jules, we have to go back. Mum needs us now."

"Did Mum call you?" she asked.

"No, I just know we have to go back now," I replied.

As we walked back into Dad's room Mum said, "Oh, Kathryn, thank God you came back, something's changed, it felt different the minute you left." I sat down and Mum asked me to give Dad healing and play the 'angel song'. I didn't want to play it as I knew Dad would die during the song. I felt it had to do with what I saw during the night. So, I deliberately played 'A Hundred Thousand Angels'.

"Not that song," she said. "The other angel song."

Julianne said, "It is okay, Mum, we can listen to this one first." The song finished and she asked for the other song again. I played that song and decided to fill out the menu form for Mum. I had Beni in my arms and as I started to fill out the form, I felt a shift in the energy. I whipped my head around and saw Dad standing beside his body. He looked as he did when he was in his thirties.

"Dad's dead," I stated.

"No, he isn't, I can hear him breathing," Mum replied.

I walked over and checked for a pulse and there wasn't one. "Yes, he is, Mum, that is the breathing tube making that noise." He was gone.

Tony took Chloe out into the garden to share the sad news, and as soon as he told her a large feather dropped on her foot. She started squealing, "He is here! Grandad is here! He gave me the feather."

Then we heard that when the staff opened the reception door at the motel he owned, a swarm of yellow butterflies were at the door.

A few days before Dad's funeral, I was with Mum as she watered the garden that Dad made for her before he got sick. She was upset because Dad had not come to her. I explained that her grief was so heavy that he was not getting through to her. Just at that moment a butterfly landed on her arm that was holding the hose.

"Look Mum, Dad is here!" I gently said.

"Where is he, can you see him?" she anxiously asked.

"Look, there is a butterfly on your arm." She looked at her arm, and then the butterfly fluttered from her arm to her chest in the vicinity of her heart. Dad had fulfilled his promise.

Months later Chloe and I were in the car on the way to a Zumba class, when she asked me, "Do you think Grandad is with us in the car?"

"Yes, I think he is," I replied.

Three tracks into our Zumba class, in the middle of a track, one of Dad's favourite songs, 'Eagle Rock' suddenly blasted through the

Messages From Beyond: Proof of Life After Death

speakers. Chloe and I looked at each other, as Dad loved dancing to this song, it was even his ringtone. The Zumba instructor got flustered and raced over to change the track as 'Eagle Rock' was not usually played at this Zumba class. The instructor apologised and started the correct track again. Then 'Eagle Rock' started playing for a second time during the next track. The instructor could not work out why it was happening as that song was not on the playlist, and she didn't think it was even in her music library! Dad had answered Chloe's question. For a non-believer, Dad was doing a really good job of giving proof of life after death.

The spirit world are all around us, and they love to let you know that they are here. They can use many forms of communication, e.g. lights flashing, electronics malfunctioning, symbolic reminders. Your loved ones in spirit will take any opportunity they can to communicate with you. I have known of people finding coins as their dad was a coin collector when he was alive, and that was how he was now sending messages. Your loved one's favourite song might play randomly. You might even have a random memory pop into your mind. If you look for the signs I am sure you will find them.

Readings

If life were predictable it would cease to be life and be without flavour

—Eleanor Roosevelt.

I love having a psychic reading and witnessing how other psychic mediums work. You might ask why would I want to have a reading with another psychic, when I am already one? I find that it is always lovely to connect to your loved ones through another medium. Sure, I can connect, but then I sometimes wonder if I am receiving what I want to hear. If I have an issue that I am struggling with it is always good to get a second opinion. Reading for myself in those situations is not ideal as I really can't be totally objective when I am invested in the outcome. I would be telling myself that everything is going to be fine! That was one of the main reasons that I developed *The Modern Oracle* decks, so that I could not only obtain accurate answers for myself, but also for those that I am considered 'too close' to. With families it can be difficult to read for them as you already know a lot about them, and they tend to assume that another family member has already mentioned it.

For some people, with age they become more intuitive and it is hard for their friends and families to get their head around the fact that all of a sudden you are psychic, and reading for other people. It was not sudden, for most; it has been building up to this point.

When you read for someone, you are giving them guidance as to what could be their potential future or outcome. I say potential, as they choose if they accept the guidance or disregard it. You are advising them of a path that is available to them. What the client does after they leave you is up to them. For example, I once advised a man who was dating many women all at the same time that he was about to be found out if he didn't stop dating them all. When my client caught up with me a year later he confided that he had sent one of the women to see me for a reading, and that I had told her that her partner was seeing many other women, all at the same time. After hearing this news, the lady then 'stalked' him, and upon discovering proof of his actions, she then advised each of the other women. The next time I saw this client, he said, "I have a bone to pick with you."

"Why?" I asked.

"I sent someone to see you and you apparently told her that her partner was seeing many other women," he replied.

"Well, how did that work out for you and what did you think would happen if you sent her to me?" I asked with attitude.

"She somehow found the other women and they all dumped me, but it's all good," he laughingly replied.

Readings

"Sorry about that, I hope you have learnt your lesson," I replied with a smile. In hindsight he was able to laugh about it now. He went on to find the love of his life and is now happily married.

It can be a scary step when you decide to read for others in a professional capacity and be paid for your time. We all want our readings to be accurate and our clients to be happy, but there are certain responsibilities that come with the job, including confidentiality. I include below the guidance that I have always followed and also teach to my students.

- Meditate as much as you can—even five minutes is better than nothing. Many people have busy lives and can find it hard to find the time
- Follow your intuition and TRUST! Let go of fear and have a go: nothing ventured, nothing gained! We all have to start somewhere
- Don't compare your gift to anyone else's
- Always protect yourself energetically and stay 'grounded'—exercise, eat a meal, be human, hug a tree, be physical
- Work with integrity at all times and respect others
- Practise on willing friends and family but don't read for anyone without their permission; they have their right to privacy
- Don't expect to be right all the time. Only God or whoever you pray to is, and people have free will. There is no one in any field of work that is 100% correct all the time. So, don't take it personally if you do get it wrong
- Set boundaries and stick to them. It is not wise to become a psychic ATM and others to become dependent on you, as it can be very draining and deplete your energy. There should be an exchange of energy for your time, e.g. money or a swap of services

- You don't have to prove your gifts to anyone and don't become a party trick. There will always be a sceptic somewhere that will want to challenge you. Everyone is entitled to their own beliefs. I find when someone mentions that I am a psychic at a party the cheating partners make themselves scarce and the rest put you on the spot to read for them or ask if you can see their deceased grandmother
- Unless you are 100% sure, it is not advisable to deliver bad or upsetting news, e.g. that someone is going to die! It is not good to share news of that kind, and then for the client to go home, full of dread, waiting for it to happen
- Don't be a scary psychic that people are afraid to go to. Your client should leave with hope and a plan to move forward gained from your guidance
- It is always good to obtain client testimonials, as evidence or proof that you're on the right track. Testimonials can be confidence building. Whenever you start to doubt yourself, read back through the testimonials, to eliminate your doubt. The client would not have written them if they were not impressed with you
- **Always** be confidential. Never discuss anyone else's reading. If you can't be trusted to be confidential then your clients will not return to you for a reading or refer your services to others

I don't usually remember anyone's readings, and they are out of my head shortly after I finish the reading. I used to think I was a psychic 'airhead' because I couldn't remember people's readings. Then I learnt that it is not my business to remember, and anyway, I don't think I have the extensive RAM like a computer. I would require a photographic memory to remember the details of all the thousands of readings I have done. Yet I have returning clients that say, "Do you remember when I last had a reading with you, and you told me 'such and such' was going to happen?"

Readings

My answer is always, "Sorry, I don't, as I have done many readings since then."

The odd time that I do remember any details from a reading, it is usually because it was something very 'different', that perhaps shocked me, and even then, I don't remember who the person was. For example, people in three-way relationships or open marriages. It is not my place to judge; I am just there to give guidance.

I read for many celebrities and the reason that they keep returning, as well as referring me to their friends and families, is because they know that I am always confidential.

Readings can be conducted from anywhere and we don't always have the ideal space to read from. I remember working at a psychic expo doing readings and I had quickly booked out for the two days. I was doing readings one after the other, with only a couple of minutes between each one, and a five-minute break scheduled after every four readings. I actually prefer to work this way as once I start, I like to stay in the energy. All was going well until a fire alarm went off. We never schedule for things like that. I continued the reading as intuitively I knew it was a false alarm, and the client was not going to budge as she wanted her reading to continue. I knew that I had to complete the readings as they had all been prepaid and I hate disappointing anyone.

Everyone was leaving the building and finally, I, too, had to leave (they wouldn't let me stay!). With the current client in tow and the next one following me, I grabbed my *Modern Oracle* decks and found a bench seat outside the building where I continued to do the booked readings. It is amazing what you can do when you have to.

As part of my training at college I was put under pressure to read in many different circumstances. I performed readings while walking through a large garden. I had sat on a chair blindfolded and read for an unknown previous person who had sat on that chair while I was out of the room. The tutor was the only one to speak to confirm the details. There were many ways that I was challenged to demonstrate what I was capable of, and this helped to build my confidence further.

Before a day of reading for clients, I **meditate and set the intention**. That is, I ask for what I want to achieve, such as a clear and accurate connection. This is an important step for you to do.

You also need to **trust the connection**, the same way a child trusts a parent. You will learn to recognise the presence of spirit. I feel a tingly warmth on my right side when connecting to my guides and helpers. When connecting to the spirit world, I feel it at the back of my neck. You will grow more confident in your ability to communicate with practice and the more knowledge you gain. You need to believe in the process and yourself as you develop.

Have **belief** that you can do it, that it is possible. Believe in yourself.
Have **faith** that you are doing it and will improve with practice.
Have the **confidence** to keep going.

Then it is important to **focus,** which is about building the energy. Creating an intensity. Clearing the path for clear direction. Clearing the mind of distractions to enable a clear reception. Like fine tuning the television station to get a clearer picture. You focus, tuning in the station until it is perfect, then you can understand what you are watching, and the sound is clearer without distortion. The interference is gone.

If you wish, work with **tools** that 'talk' to you. You can work with tarot, oracle cards, a pendulum, palmistry, numerology, Reiki or different forms of healing. There are so many options! Be open to

Readings

trying out new tools and learning as much as you can so you can find the divination tools that resonate with you.

Always express **gratitude** for your innate psychic ability and the presence of spirit will raise your vibration and confidence. We all need to feel appreciated and to appreciate what we have. By being grateful, you become open to more of which you are thankful. Also, when people feel appreciated, they can be motivated to assist more. Your guides interpret your gratitude as permission to help you even further.

In short, you can become more psychic by being in the energy, setting the intention, believing in the process, trusting in yourself and practising. Read for people you don't know and ask for their feedback, so you can learn how the spirit world communicates with you. With practice comes confidence, know-how and progress. Without even realising it, you are already becoming more psychic.

Mystery Crystal Exercise

The following exercise can help you to develop the practice of tuning into a crystal in preparation for psychometry and experiencing different energies. My students love this exercise. You will need a selection of crystals to add to a bag for the following exercise. This is a good exercise to do when you want to practise distinguishing different energies.

Exercise:

Close your eyes.
Relax and take three deep breaths in and out.
Select a crystal out of the bag.
Hold the crystal gently, and with your eyes remaining closed tune in to the energy of the crystal for a couple of minutes.
Now keep the crystal in your non-dominant, closed hand for the duration of the exercise.
When you feel ready, open your eyes and without looking at the crystal, answer the following questions in your psychic journal.

- *How does the crystal's energy feel?*
- *What thoughts go through your mind as you hold this crystal?*
- *What colour do you think the crystal is?*
- *What part of the body do you feel the crystal connects to?*
- *Did you see any images?*
- *What healing properties do you think the crystal has?*
- *What crystal do you think you are holding, e.g. amethyst, tourmaline, etc.?*

Once you have answered the above questions you can look at your crystal and identify it, e.g. citrine, rose quartz, etc. Then use a book on crystals or google about the crystal to check your answers. This exercise helps you to connect, focus and build your confidence with the use of psychometry. Psychometry is the practice of reading the energy of an object or connecting to the owner of the object while it is held in your hand. Sometimes a client will bring in something that belonged to a deceased loved one to assist in a closer connection.

Psychic Tools

Give ordinary people the right tools, and they will design and build the most extraordinary things
—Neil Gershenfeld.

A tool is anything used as a means of accomplishing a task or purpose. Different tools are used in many professions and everyone uses some sort of tool throughout their lives.

Tools can make a task easier, quicker and more accurate. For example, a doctor uses tools to enable a more accurate diagnosis, e.g. a stethoscope, X-ray machine, etc. Fences can be built a lot quicker and easier with the use of a nail gun instead of a hammer. Do you see where I am going with this? I would prefer to use an electric beater than a wooden spoon to make a sponge cake or meringues. Tools are designed to make your job easier. Psychics also benefit from the use of tools to enhance their readings, and for many other reasons. There is a broad selection of tools to choose from depending on what works right for you.

Your psychic senses are your personal intuitive tools that I discussed in more detail earlier in this book. They are:

> **Clairvoyance**—clear seeing
> **Clairsentience**—clear feeling
> **Clairaudience**—clear hearing
> **Clairalience** or **Clairolfaction**—clear smelling
> **Clairgustance**—clear tasting
> **Claircognizance**—clear knowing

When I conduct readings, I connect to my spirit team and then start talking, delivering the information that I am receiving; sometimes I incorporate a tool into the reading. The tools I favour are the two decks I created: *The Modern Oracle* deck and *The Modern Oracle of Essential Oils* deck. I have especially found these decks are beneficial for when I am reading for myself and loved ones.

For psychics it can be difficult to read for yourself or anyone that you are close to. The reason being is that sometimes you can be too invested in the outcome and it can be difficult to remain objective. If anything negative is suggested, I will immediately want to reject it. There are also times where it can be construed that you had prior knowledge, e.g. you had been previously confided in. For example, I once told my sister that I was hearing (using my clairaudience) that she was pregnant. As she looked at me she asked with disbelief, "Did Mum tell you? I told her not to tell anyone." Of course, Mum hadn't told me. Yet, if I used *The Modern Oracle* cards and the 'pregnancy' card was drawn, it is more believable, especially for those that I am close to, as the card has provided confirmation.

Psychic Tools

When working with your psychic energy, there are many tools that you can use to enhance a psychic reading, healing, energy work or to facilitate greater focus. Below I have listed some of the many tools available. There are way too many for me to list all of them in this book. As you work with the tools you may soon develop a preference and your own style of how you work with each of them.

- Crystal balls—used for scrying, using your clairvoyance
- Pendulums—divination tool for a 'yes' or 'no' answer
- Tarot cards—for guidance
- Oracle cards—for guidance
- Crystals—for their energetic properties, including healing
- Runes—for guidance
- Palm reading—(chiromancy) the art of reading lines on hands
- Colour—used for healing, reading auras
- Numerology—the study of numbers in your life
- Psychometry—the practice of reading the energy of an object

Many psychics love to collect different tools. I know of psychics that have vast collections of different oracle and tarot decks. Many have huge crystal collections. I love crystals, and work with them a lot. I use some of the larger ones to energetically charge my 'Psychic Enhancer' oil, as part of the creative process. I like to always have a channelling crystal nearby when I am working and I collect heart-shaped crystals, due to the heart shape being a symbol of love and because I was born on Valentine's Day. I believe you not only get the healing benefits and power of the crystals, but you get the love too. My husband jokingly says we have a rock quarry in our house, but it is not true. We just have a lot of crystals. In fact, the last crystal that I 'adopted', I told him it was a fruit bowl to get it in the house (after he told me not to bring any more home) and he took me literally and now he puts fruit in it.

Many years ago, as my awareness started to resurface strongly, I had a healing massage with a lady called Sue who owned a new age shop. The shop had an amazing energy and was definitely haunted. During the massage Sue's grandmother (in spirit) came through strongly. She wanted to connect with her granddaughter. I ignored her at first, due to fear of being wrong. What if her grandmother was still alive, and I was communicating with someone else? Her grandmother continued to encourage me to deliver her message for her granddaughter. I knew she wasn't going to give up. Finally, I gave up and found the courage and confidence to communicate what she wanted to say. Sue was amazed, and frankly, I was too, as I was still struggling with trusting my psychic gift.

When I went to pay for the massage, Sue suggested I buy a book on chakras, as she held out a book in my direction. I clearly remember to this day how naive I was back then. I didn't know much about chakras and I stupidly replied, "Maybe another time, as I don't think I'm ready for them now." Which now causes me to chuckle, as at that time, I thought they were some weird mystical belief. Obviously I was not ready to learn about chakras. Little did I know as I continued on my spiritual journey that the 'chakra' word would continue to pop up everywhere from that point on until I embraced the importance of chakras.

What Are Chakras?

A chakra is believed to be a centre of activity that receives, assimilates and expresses life force energy. Each chakra is like a spiral of energy relating to the others. Together the chakras form the energy system of our body.

It is typical for chakras to be depicted in two ways, either flower-like or wheel-like, with either having a specific number of petals or spokes.

It is believed that we all have many chakras. The seven main chakras are located along the spine, beginning at the base of the spinal column and moving upward to the top of the skull. Their balanced state is responsible for our healthy physical and mental being.

Let me tell you the names and locations of the seven main chakras of the human body. Visualising your body from **feet to head**, we have the following chakras:

Root/Base Chakra—'I Have'

Location: Base of spine and the pubic bone, positioned downwards towards the ground

Colour: Red, symbolised by a lotus with four petals

Purpose: An energy centre relating to physical existence, our will to live, instinct, security and survival, e.g. earning money

Key issues involve sexuality, lust, obsession, stability and sense of security

Ideally: This chakra brings us health, prosperity, security and dynamic presence

Sacral Chakra—Desire 'I Feel, and I Want'

Location: Behind and just below the navel, abdomen, the sacrum

Colour: Orange, symbolised by a lotus with six petals

Purpose: It is related to our sexuality and creativity. Creativity in all forms of life from children to art. Physical satisfaction such as eating, drinking and sex

Key issues involve relationships, violence, addictions, basic emotional needs, pleasure, reproduction, creativity, joy and enthusiasm

Ideally: This chakra brings us fluidity, grace, depth of feeling, sexual fulfillment and the ability to accept change

Solar Plexus Chakra—'I Can'
Location: Above the navel in the solar plexus, the base of the ribs. Related to metabolic and digestive systems, adrenal glands

Colour: Yellow, symbolised by a lotus with ten petals

Purpose: It is related to our personal power and energy, our intuition, 'gut feeling'. Assimilates experiences and determines what is working for you, giving confidence and achievement. It is where you feel excitement and fear

Key issues involve personal power, fear, anxiety, opinion formation, introversion, and transition from simple or base emotions to complex, digestion, personal power and expansiveness

Ideally: This chakra brings us energy, effectiveness and spontaneity

Heart Chakra—'I Love'
Location: Centre of the chest, related to the thymus (immune system)

Colour: Green (pink centre), symbolised by the lotus flower with 12 petals

Purpose: It is related to love and will

Key issues involve complex emotions, compassion, tenderness, equilibrium, rejection, devotion, wellbeing, circulation, passion and unconditional love for self and others

Ideally: This chakra allows us to love deeply, feel compassion, and have a deep sense of peace and centredness

Throat Chakra—'I Say'
Location: Throat area, related to the thyroid gland which produces a thyroid hormone responsible for growth and maturation

Colour: Light blue or turquoise, symbolised by a lotus with 16 petals

Purpose: It is related to giving and receiving and telling your truth

Key issues involve sound, clear communication, self-expression, fluent thought, independence, truth and principles

Ideally: This chakra allows us to clearly communicate truthfully

Brow Chakra/Third eye—'I See'
Location: Centre of the forehead, related to the light sensitive pineal gland that produces the hormone melatonin which regulates sleep and awakening

Colour: Indigo or deep blue, symbolised by a lotus with two petals

Purpose: Your psychic centre of inspiration and awareness

Key issues involve access of intuition, trust of inner guidance, clarity on an intuitive level and clairvoyance

Ideally: This chakra when healthy allows us to see clearly, in effect, letting us 'see the big picture'

Crown Chakra—'I Am'
Location: Top of head, crown, relates to the pituitary gland which secretes hormones to communicate to the rest of the endocrine system and also connects the central nervous system via the hypothalamus

Colour: Violet/white, symbolised by a lotus with one thousand petals

Purpose: It is how we get our direct knowing and integrate ourselves with spirituality. Connection to the life force, spiritual energy

Key issues involve inner wisdom, meditation, universal consciousness and unity, being-ness and the release of karma

Ideally: This chakra brings us knowledge, wisdom, understanding and spiritual connection

It is important to have balanced chakras, as whichever chakra is out of whack you will see a deficit, meaning that part of your life can be found to be lacking in some way.

To end this chapter, I will tell you a true story. I had just finished teaching a workshop, and one of the subjects was about chakras. I had promised the students that I would check their chakras and balance them at the end of the workshop. A student approached me and gave me permission to check her chakras with my pendulum.

"Your root chakra is out of balance," I said to her.

Before I could check the next chakra she yelled out to her partner across the room,

"Hey, hon, my rooting chakra is not working! We are not doing enough rooting! You better get yours checked out too."

She then looked at me with a wicked glint in her eye and asked if I would check his as well.

By this time, I was struggling to keep a straight face. I quickly explained that it wasn't exactly a 'rooting' chakra. She smilingly looked at me and exclaimed, "I know!" She had said that to embarrass her partner. By now, everyone in the room was laughing with her. They all got the joke.

Exercise on Psychometry:

Psychometry is a clairsentient skill. It is the art of reading the aura of an inanimate object, usually by holding it. You tap into the aura of the object and pick up on the energy of one of its previous owners. Everything has an aura (an energy field). The more frequent an object is used, the more likely it is to have a strong aura.

Some psychics use psychometry to trace missing persons. The psychic tunes into the energy of a possession belonging to the missing person and may be able to assist in providing information to help trace that person.

To be able to measure your accuracy in the following exercise, you must work with objects whose history is known, but not by you.

This exercise will assist in developing the practice of tuning into an object, e.g. a piece of jewellery, keys, a book.

Exercise:

- Relax and take three deep breaths in and out
- Set the intention that you desire to connect with the object you are holding
- Open yourself to the Universe (visualise white light beaming down from the Universe and filling your body, and then expanding your aura)
- Hold the object and sit quietly with it for a couple of minutes. You can close your eyes if it makes it easier and improves your concentration
- Breathe normally and tune into the object. Take note of the thoughts, emotions, images and sensations that come to you
- Start speaking and say whatever comes to mind. Do not allow fear to block the flow of you receiving information
- If you feel nothing, then ask yourself questions about the object, one question at a time, allowing time for the answers

Signs and Synchronicity: Show Me a Sign

> In every moment, the universe is whispering to you. You're constantly surrounded by signs, coincidences, and synchronicities, all aimed at propelling you in the direction of your destiny
>
> —Denise Linn.

Have you ever heard someone say, "That is just a coincidence, it doesn't mean anything?"
Have you ever thought there has to be more to a series of coincidences? I believe there is, and it seems that a series of 'coincidences' become a 'synchronicity'.

The Modern Oracle

I have always determined that a synchronicity is a sign of confirmation from the Universe that you are on the right path and heading in the right direction. A sceptic may refer to a synchronicity as a coincidence and therefore there is no reason for the occurrence. Below are the meanings of both words from *Oxford Languages*.

Synchronicity: the simultaneous occurrence of events which appear significantly related but have no discernible causal connection—*Oxford Languages*.

Coincidence: a remarkable concurrence of events or circumstances without apparent causal connection—*Oxford Languages*.

Many times, there are occasions that occur in our lives that we explain by saying that it was 'just a coincidence'. I prefer to say that it was how it was meant to be. That you are on the right path and heading in the right direction and these are the tell-tale signs to prove it. Another synchronicity can be certain events happening on the same day; e.g. my parents and Tony's parents were both married on the same day in different parts of Australia. I believe this confirmed that Tony was meant for me. My cousin died on my father's birthday. One of my favourite tutors shared the same birthday as my father, and this confirmed that he was the right tutor for me. My nephew was born on the same day my father died. Tony's mother is born in the same month as my mother and Tony's father is born in the same month as my father. Our dog Ted shared the same birthday as one of my best friends, Marilla, and he originally had the same name as her husband.

One night, Tony and I were driving back to the Sunshine Coast in the pouring rain from Brisbane after visiting my dad in hospital. It had been a long day and we were both tired. I mentioned to him that my neck felt like it was 'out' and I needed to see a good chiropractor. No sooner had the words left my mouth than I looked up and there

Signs and Synchronicity: Show Me a Sign

on the corner of a roundabout was a sign saying 'Chiropractor'. Not being familiar with the area I had not seen that sign before, so I didn't manage to get the details; however, this felt like it was a sign.

The next morning, I awoke feeling that I should see a chiropractor sooner rather than later. I google searched for chiropractors in the area hoping to be able to find the one that I saw on the sign the previous night. I felt that it was no coincidence that the sign appeared before me as soon as I mentioned my need. I did not even know the name of the street where I had seen the sign and google had brought up many listings. I thought, *Well, I am just going to have to use my intuition and be guided on this decision.*

I rang a number from the listings and asked if they had any appointments available. They had only one appointment left at 12.30 p.m., as someone had just cancelled, so I quickly claimed it. When I arrived for my appointment it turned out to be the same business that I had seen on the sign. The resident chiropractor was on leave and as it happened his replacement was very spiritual and amazing. I felt like I had received a 'healing' session from a very thorough chiropractor and unusually, I felt better straight away instead of days after the treatment. I really believe synchronicity came into play, for I saw the sign the moment I made the request and then unknowingly selected the place I saw on the sign, when I really did not have a clue.

Another example of signs and synchronicity occurred when I was walking along the River Thames in England with a good friend and moaning about how unhappy I was that I was doing the Fast Diet by Dr Michael Mosely, while I was on holidays. I wanted a break from dieting, but intuitively knew I should continue. Other times when I had come over for college, I had taken home with me three kilos of excess baggage on my body, with most of it on my arse. So, I asked the Universe to show me a sign if I was meant to continue the Fast

Diet. Amazingly, less than an hour later we walked past Dr Michael Mosely filming beside the Thames. There was my sign, and I had my answer. Much to my disappointment, it seemed that I needed to continue on the Fast Diet. I was happy that I continued the diet as this time only my suitcase gained weight.

A lot of people receive symbolic signs as a form of confirmation: a language that the Universe uses to communicate with you. For example, a snake to me is a symbol of betrayal or a warning, that says 'watch out' or 'don't progress any further'. That doesn't mean to say that it has the same meaning for everyone else.

I have had snakes turn up on my doorstep, and then, a betrayal followed. I have even had a snake wrap itself around a door handle when we were looking at buying a new home. My husband had set up a time for us to view the house with the real estate agent. As we pulled up in front of the house, I had a funny feeling, and it wasn't a comforting one. "I don't want to see this house, I don't like it," I stated to Tony. "This is not the house for us," I added.

"Well, at least take a look at it so that we haven't wasted the agent's time," Tony replied.

We walked through and inspected the house with our young children in tow. Then went out the back door and inspected the yard as the agent did his sales pitch. As I turned around to walk back into the house, our daughter Chloe, who was only three at the time, yelled out, "Mum, there's a snake!" I looked up, and sure enough, there was a snake wrapped around the door handle. I grabbed our kids and took them back to our car. I was not going to go back into that house, and I certainly would not buy it. The snake was a warning and sure enough, six months later that house flooded.

Signs and Synchronicity: Show Me a Sign

At certain times in my life when I had felt unsure, or needed confirmation on a decision, I have asked the spirit world to show me a sign that I am on the right path.

One night when I was driving home, I encountered a white owl in the middle of the road not far from my house. I had not seen a white owl before, and I stopped the car to give it a chance to move. It didn't! So, I drove around the owl and turned the corner into the street where I lived. As I arrived at my driveway, there, sitting on the top of the tall gates, was the white owl, looking at me.

The owl then remained on the gates watching me throughout the whole process of getting in and out of the car to open and close the gates and drive the car through. I was so close that I could have reached up and touched the owl. Before I drove the car into the garage, I raced into the house to get my family to come and have a look.

They were amazed about what had happened. I finally drove the car into the garage and with that the owl flew to the top of the garage, where it stayed and continued to stare at me for a few more minutes. I knew this had to be a sign. The meaning I was taught about the owl is the 'getting of wisdom' and 'messages from spirit'. This made sense as this visit was straight after returning from my first visit to the Arthur Findlay College. In many countries the symbolic meaning of the owl is different; for instance, in Greece the owl is a sign of good luck. I encourage you to journal your symbolic meanings and what the symbol means to you as you learn them.

Exercise:

In your psychic journal find a place to list what your symbolic meanings are; e.g. When I see a snake, then you are warning me to watch out (this does not include if you visit a zoo!). This then confirms your belief and your way of communicating with the Universe. It is like learning a new language, your 'spirit' language. Not everyone will have the same meaning for different symbols. It is up to you to work out how the spirit world is communicating with you.

Animal Communication: If I Could Talk to the Animals

Until one has loved an animal, a part of one's soul remains unawakened
—Anatole France.

Do you believe that people can communicate with animals? I never did, but it didn't stop me from chattering away to them. I just didn't believe that they would talk to me!

I never would have believed for one minute that I would be able to communicate with animals. I love animals and I am an avid dog lover. I just adore dogs and if we could, I am sure we would have more than two dogs. I was never allowed to have a dog as a child and as soon as I left home, I got a dog.

In the early days of my spiritual development, whenever I was at a zoo, I would look at an animal, then focus on them intently and say in my mind, *If you can hear me, look at me now.* Sometimes they did, and I would think that was a fluke, a coincidence. I wasn't very confident! A lot of the times they ignored me, which led me to deduce that it wasn't working and I couldn't communicate with them. So, when the opportunity came up to attend an 'Animal Communication' workshop, I was there. I didn't know what to expect and I really didn't expect to be able to do it.

The first exercise we were all asked to do was to connect to this beautiful white horse that the owner had recently adopted and write down all the things we could about the horse's life, especially its history. The previous owner had communicated the history of the horse to the new owner. This would enable us to verify most of any information that we received from the horse. This exercise was really putting me out of my comfort zone, but I knew that if I didn't try, I would never know if I could do it. It was a big exercise in trusting the information that I received and hoping the horse wasn't a liar! Ha, ha.

I looked at the horse and, in my mind, I politely asked, *Can you tell me about yourself?* I got nothing! Then I decided to visualise myself sending love to this beautiful creature. I was beaming love to the horse and asking it questions in my head. Then slowly the information started coming through. I realised then and there that as the horse did not know me, why would it want to tell me anything. Like a person, the horse needed to feel comfortable with me before it confided in me. Then there was the fact that all the other students were hoping to connect at the same time with the horse. Imagine a roomful of people all talking over the top of each other and expecting you to answer them all at the same time.

With my love beaming at the horse, I broke through a barrier and started to learn about the hard life this horse had experienced. I wrote

Animal Communication: If I Could Talk to the Animals

down his age, how many owners he had previously had. His likes and dislikes. How he grieved because he saw a horse that he shared a paddock with getting shot and then die. How he had been mistreated when he was with a previous owner, and how now he was adored by his new owner and her family. How he had gotten attached to their other pets. How he liked to eat with the family dogs on the verandah, as well as much more. When I stopped writing, I thanked the horse and then thought, *I wonder if I have just written down a load of 'horse shit'*. I was not confident at all.

The tutor, who had come all the way from the UK, went around the group asking each student to read out what they had discovered about this horse. I remember thinking, *Crap, it looks like I am going to be last*. Why did that seem like a problem to me? Because maybe there would be nothing left to say by the time it was my turn. Going last actually ended up working in my favour. A few students presented some really accurate information. Some of them let their fear block them and decided to 'play it safe'. They were not confident enough to take a risk in case they got it wrong. They were the ones that talked about what the horse liked to eat and funnily enough it just happened to be the same food that all horses like to eat. How he liked to be scratched, and general horse stuff, which I didn't have much knowledge of, having never been around horses during my life to date. It is quite easy to doubt yourself and therefore not take any risks. It is a big thing to put yourself out there and can take a lot of courage, and to quote Alfred Lord Tennyson: "It is better to have tried and failed than never tried at all."

When it came time for my turn, I took a deep breath and started to read out the details that I had written down. They were very specific details and I was taking a big risk, as most of my list was different from the previous students' lists. So, there was no way that anyone could assume I was just saying what had previously been said. To my surprise, I got it all correct! Both the tutor and the horse's owner were also surprised about the amount of accurate details. I was both shocked and delighted. When I returned home and gleefully told my husband about my success, he humorously replied, "Probably not a good thing to tell too many people as they might think you're crazy!" It seemed he had concerns about me being perceived as 'crazy'. Funny thing was, I wasn't worried at all.

I have found that I am not anything like 'Dr Dolittle', a fictional character that could talk to animals. My mind isn't full of animal chatter whenever I am near an animal. It only spontaneously happens if the animal seeks me out, or if I deliberately tune in with the intention to connect. With my own animals, I had always thought that maybe it's all in my mind a lot of the time, as I was too close to them and the things coming into my head could be construed as prior knowledge.

When our much-loved Border Collie, Macca, died, I had actually predicted it would happen. Whenever my husband and I had to go away for business, my Uncle George and Aunty Joy would move into our home to look after our children and pets; we were so blessed. One day, with feelings of dread, I sadly mentioned to my Uncle George that I thought Macca was going to die soon and that Tony and I would not be home when it happened. I showed him where to bury him if he did die while Tony and I were away.

"Is he sick?" he asked.

"Not that I know of, it is just a feeling that I have," I replied. Macca was only ten years old and we were only aware that he had a bit of arthritis which had come from his love of kicking a basketball. I myself also thought that he might have had a bit of dementia. Macca had recently had his annual check-up and the vet was happy with him. A few weeks later Tony and I went away for business and thankfully

Animal Communication: If I Could Talk to the Animals

nothing happened. My uncle questioned me to see if I was still sure that Macca was going to die, as he was very worried. I was hoping that I could be wrong!

Weeks later Macca died while Tony and I were away in Sydney. My Uncle George said that he was perfectly fine the night before, and then they found him dead at the front door when they went to feed him. There was no apparent reason for his death, but my uncle thought that it could have been a snake bite. Our family was devastated and so was our other dog Bozzie (our Lhasa Apso/Maltese cross) who grieved heavily, for a long time. He would even visit his grave down the bottom of the backyard overlooking a lagoon.

Five years later Bozzie died. On the day he died, he had what I would call his best day. As usual he came and got me to take him for a walk on the nearby beach. He loved to walk but this day, we didn't get very far before he decided to turn around and go home. He was also walking slower. I fed him his favourite meal and he seemed fine. I went to bed and he stayed up late to watch TV with Tony as he liked to do. I was reading in bed and Tony rushed into the bedroom, holding Bozzie, and said, "Something is wrong, I think Bozzie is sick."

At that moment Macca, our deceased Border Collie, appeared in the room and put his paws on our bed, something he never did when he was alive, as he was an outside dog. Macca told me that Bozzie was dying, and he had come to take him and would look after him.

I said to Tony, "Bozzie is dying."

"How do you know?" he asked.

"Because Macca is here to be with him and take him away," I said with great sadness. We were both sobbing and cradling him as he died in our arms a couple of hours later. I then saw him leave his body and walk off with Macca. For three years I would tear up every time I thought of him. Our family was devastated. Interestingly, Bella, our five-year-old Shih Tzu cross, did not appear to grieve the way Bozzie had when Macca died. Then I realised why. Bella could still see him! When I would see Bozzie in spirit, Bella would be looking in the same direction as I was.

It is not unusual for deceased pets to come through in a reading with messages for their loved ones. I had a client visit my cottage for a reading with a shopping bag in his hand that he placed at his feet. In his reading I connected to his recently departed dog, and the client was reduced to tears. At the end of the session he tearfully picked up the bag and showed me the contents. The bag was full of his dog's toys. He was hoping that his dog would come through, especially if he brought the dog's toys with him.

Recently I was visiting my hairdresser who works from home. I had often seen her dog Bender sitting outside the screen door. He was not allowed into the house, but he loved to come in if a door was left open. One day while I was getting a haircut, my hairdresser Shelley left the room and left the door open. Bender took the opportunity to sneak in. He strolled over to me, licked my foot and sat down next to my feet, something he had never done before. I started patting him and telling him what a beautiful boy he was. Shelley walked back in and I said to her, "Bender only wants to eat one type of food, and he doesn't like what you are currently feeding him."

"Yes, he is not eating it and all other food is going straight through him," she replied.

"Well, he is telling me he doesn't like what you are feeding him, and he wants the other dog food that he likes. He tells me he is 14 years old, is that correct?"

Animal Communication: If I Could Talk to the Animals

"Yes," she replied, and added, "Looks like I will have to go back to buying that expensive dog food that he likes."

"Yes, and he also has dementia and arthritis," I said.

"Yes, he has arthritis and the dementia diagnosis does not surprise me. Yesterday he wandered down the street and went to a house he doesn't know. The owner contacted me to come and get him. He has never wandered off like that before."

Bender had chosen to communicate through me. On my last visit to Shelley, she confirmed that Bender is now happy and eating the dog food he likes.

I now know that animal communication is very real and it's not an endless one-way conversation with me doing all the talking. Psychic mediums who are animal lovers can find it a lot easier to learn to communicate with animals than others who don't have an affinity with animals.

If you are an animal lover, you might like to have a go at communicating with animals. It could take some time and a lot of practice. It all depends on how dedicated you are, and if it is one of your strengths.

When I teach, I like to break the steps down, so they are easy to understand and uncomplicated. This exercise is a simplified version. How long it takes for you to be successful at it depends on how dedicated you are and how often you practise. It also helps if you have an affinity with animals. Not everyone will master it, but you won't know unless you try. Give it a go; you never know, you just might be successful.

Here is a quick outline of the steps that I use:

1. Relax and centre yourself.
2. Take a few deep breaths.
3. Set the intention that you wish to connect with the animal you wish to communicate with.
4. Send a steady stream of love beaming out to the animal; visualise it as a beam of pink light.
5. Then speak either in your mind or out loud to the animal.
6. Persevere and keep trying.
7. Remember to thank the animal.
8. Clear and disconnect (stop the beam of light) from the animal.

Remember, sometimes the animal is not wanting to talk to you, especially if it doesn't know or trust you. If you can, take time to make friends first, so the animal can get used to your energy. Know that some animals are just plain obstinate, like some animals in the zoo, e.g. monkeys! The animal has a choice whether it communicates with you. You might want to practise by asking for the animal to look at you. Keep repeating that request until the animal responds.

Ley Lines and Sacred Sites

If you want to find the secrets of the universe, think in terms of energy, frequency and vibration
—Nikola Tesla.

I want to give you an introduction to ley lines as they can be quite significant to your spiritual journey. As this is not a book on ley lines and energy centres, I will only be giving you a brief glimpse of the basic understandings surrounding this ancient knowledge. I also don't profess to be an expert on ley lines and energy centres. However, I have experienced the energetics of these ley lines, dream lines or dragon lines, as they are referred to in different cultures, as well as the energy centres.

A handful of years ago, I didn't know much about them at all. What I do know is that whenever I am in the presence of an energy centre, ley line or vortex, I become aware of a change in the surrounding energy, and a shift in me. I also feel that my psychic skills sometimes become slightly stronger soon after. It feels like a recharge and update of my skill set. Once I became aware of this effect on me, I set out to discover other energy centres to test my theory, and hopefully elevate my skills further.

What Is a Ley Line?

I will quote from *Oxford Languages*:
A ley line is a supposed straight line connecting three or more prehistoric or ancient sites, sometimes regarded as the line of a former track and associated by some with lines of energy and other paranormal phenomena.

Ley lines are believed to be energy lines that criss-cross the earth and align with ancient sites and often energy channels. They are also known as Mother Earth's Energy Currents.

Where ley lines intersect are believed to be high points of energy and coincidentally home to some of the most sacred sites, including Stonehenge, the Egyptian Pyramids and Machu Picchu. Stonehenge is supposedly positioned at the centre of a hub, or network, of ley lines, making Stonehenge an energy portal or a place of power. Many doubt the existence of ley lines and energy portals until they experience the effects for themselves. I was one of those people and once again said to my spirit team, "If this is so, then prove it!"

Dowsing can be used to prove the presence of a ley line. Dowsing is a technique used for divination when searching for ley lines or anything invisible by observing the motion of a divining tool that will move unaided to test energy, e.g. dowsing rods and pendulums. I use dowsing rods to measure energy and how it expands. I mainly identify a vortex by a change in energy. Vortexes are thought to be swirling centres of energy that contain more energy than normal.

Sedona, Arizona, is known to have four major vortexes, and I was determined to go there to check them out. I set the goal, and then that goal was achieved while on a trip to the USA. Tony and I decided to hire a car and drive the scenic route from Phoenix to Sedona. When we checked into our accommodation, we were given a map that showed the locations of the vortexes. We selected to go to the 'Airport Mesa' vortex which boasted scenic views in nearly every direction. We parked the car in the designated car park and followed the trail to the vortex. We didn't see a sign that said, 'vortex here on this spot', but as soon as we entered the vortex, I felt the energy change. I experienced a gentle buzzing feeling on parts of my arms. There was also further proof of the vortex. The juniper trees growing in the vortex were twisted and the juniper trees outside the vortex were straight. We also discovered that whenever we were in the vortex, Tony's ears would ring. This really confirmed it for Tony, as he particularly loved his new special 'super-power' that seemed to give him the ability to detect vortexes.

Twisted Juniper tree, Sedona, Arizona

Ley Lines and Sacred Sites

The Chakras of the Earth

Mother Earth is said to have seven major chakras (energy centres), which are major power points of the planet. It is believed that it is beneficial to visit these places as the energy frequency in our bodies becomes aligned with the energy of the earth's chakras, and can produce a powerful spiritual experience. I will list these chakras and their location below.

Root Chakra—Mt. Shasta, California, USA
Believed to be the base of Mother Earth's energy system

Sacral Chakra—Lake Titicaca, Peru and Bolivia, South America

Solar Plexus Chakra—Uluru and Kata Tijuta, Northern Territory, Australia

Heart Chakra—Is a dual chakra and therefore covers two areas. Glastonbury and Shaftesbury, England, including Stonehenge, as well as the surrounding areas of Glastonbury, Somerset, Shaftesbury, Dorset and Maui, Hawaii all form the heart chakra of Mother Earth

Throat Chakra—A combination of three important sites: The Great Pyramid and Mt. Sinai, Egypt; Mt. of Olives, Jerusalem, Israel

Third Eye Chakra—Western Europe. This chakra is the only chakra which can shift locations on the Earth, supposedly due to the rotation of the Earth on its axis. Currently it is at Glastonbury, Shaftesbury, Western Europe

Crown Chakra—Mt. Kailas (Himalayan Mountains) Tibet

Whenever I travel to England, I am always drawn to visit Glastonbury. I am hooked on the place, and I always feel excited about each visit.

With its amazing energy, and a main street full of new age shops to explore, I could spend weeks there. I find that for me there is always a sense of 'coming home', and I would expect that the reason is because at this time and place, Glastonbury is situated in both the heart and third eye chakras.

Avebury is another site that I love and there is a larger 'henge' than Stonehenge resting there. At the time of writing of this book, you could freely walk in amongst the stones and feel their energy.

Another 'energy' incident occurred during one of my visits to Hawaii. I was staying in Waikiki and doing readings from our hotel room. My manager, Emma, called to ask if one of the clients that was booked in for a reading could pick me up and take me to visit a sacred site as well as do her reading.

Once I was in the client's car, I started the reading, which was probably the longest one I have ever done, as it was ongoing for the majority of the time we were together. The drive took us on a multi-lane highway that went between two majestic lush green mountains. I was still reading for the client as we stopped at a set of traffic lights. My head started to feel light as I sort of spaced out, and I felt a big shift in my energy. It was the same sort of feeling that I get whenever I am near a ley line, vortex or energy portal. Then the traffic lights didn't change for the longest time, probably about three rotations. It never seemed to be our turn to go.

My client commented, "I don't know what is happening, the lights normally don't take this long to change."

The lights finally changed to green and as we drove forward, I looked at the client and randomly said, "Sweet potatoes are my favourite food."

She looked at me in shock and said, "I have sweet potatoes cooking in my oven at home for you right now. I thought we could stop off and pick them up and while we are at my home, I was hoping that you could also bless my home?"

"I would be honoured to," I replied.

We enjoyed the freshly baked sweet potatoes by the sacred waterfall site. The flesh of the sweet potato was a vivid violet colour and delicious. I had never experienced purple sweet potatoes before. Once again, I felt an energy shift and I knew that I was at another energy 'hot spot'.

On the journey back to Waikiki with the radio playing a mainstream station in the background, I mentioned that she should work with the 'Merkabah'. Within seconds we heard the word 'Merkabah' come from the radio, and I said without hesitation, "There is your confirmation, you should work with the Merkabah." We were both shocked, as it was not a station that you would ever expect to hear the word Merkabah mentioned. My point being that when the car was between the mountains, I experienced an 'energy upgrade' and that is why we were at the lights for so long. The energy change along with the 'sweet potato' and the 'Merkabah' incidents were my confirmation of an energy upgrade.

The Merkabah is a sacred geometry symbol said to provide protection and transport your consciousness to higher dimensions. I believe that my spirit team guide me to be in the right place when it is the right time for me to receive an energy upgrade, and always after, I always feel that my gifts have grown stronger.

Exercise:

This exercise is to assist you to discover energy spots around you, and observe if there are any changes in your energy or your reaction to these areas:

- Take three deep breaths; relax and centre yourself
- Connect to the 'source' and set your intention that you wish to find energy spots and ley lines
- Using divining rods or a pendulum, walk around to find energy spots near you. Your tools will tell you once you have found them by their movement. Then seek out where they are the strongest, and the extent of the area, by the activity of your tools, i.e. the rods may move with much more intensity, and the pendulum will swing around
- You may wish to check the energy spots in areas near you and walk around and see where you get results
- Then if you get the chance you could check out well-known energy spots, like Uluru or Stonehenge. There are ley lines all over the world and maps of ley lines are available online if you do a google search of 'maps of ley lines'

Life as a Psychic

You will never follow your own inner voice until you clear up the doubts in your mind
—Roy T. Bennett.

When you are a psychic it can sometimes feel quite isolating, especially when you are trying to work out who is your friend and who just wants to take advantage of you. I consider myself lucky as I have many good, supportive friends as well as a few close ones. I have an amazing group of supportive ladies that I teach, and I also cherish their friendships. We meet on a Monday night, and I endeavour to teach them a different lesson or skill each time. You would not know it was a class, as it is always full of fun and laughter. I believe learning should be fun and when they are having fun, they are relaxed and therefore are not scared to take a risk and have a go at whatever task I set. The group is always supportive of each other and it really does make learning enjoyable. The spirit world loves it when we are happy.

Many people don't understand that most psychics do not walk around 'tuned in' all day. When I am working, I connect to the spirit world with the intention of 'turning on' my skills to work for spirit and disconnect them when I am finished. To be tuned in all the time can be like leaving a gas stove on all day, just in case you have to use it. You will eventually run out of gas.

You may find that you get approached for guidance in the supermarket; yeah, it happens! Gosh, you wouldn't go to your hairdresser in aisle 5 of the supermarket and ask them to fix your hair, and I am sure a doctor would say no to you if you were to ask them to check out a rash for you while waiting in the checkout line. You need to endeavour to have some balance in your life and by saying "no" you put up a barrier so they know your boundaries. Hand them your card and suggest they book an appointment to protect your free time.

Clients can expect you to know everything and be 100% correct at all times, even though they have the free will to change their path. I don't know of any person that is 100% correct all the time, no matter what their profession is. Hairdressers can give you a dodgy haircut, doctors can misdiagnose, mechanics can fail to fix the problem; I am sure you know where I am going with this. A psychic is the only person in the world that is expected to be correct all the time. You will also discover that there are people that, no matter what guidance you give them, in their head they hear what they want to hear or may readily identify the messages or signs themselves.

As a psychic, I can tell you that I don't always know what is going to happen, and sometimes it is difficult to interpret the messages that come through. I remember a week before September 11 (9/11) happened, I got a wave of fear overwhelm me. I remember turning to Tony and saying, "Something bad is going to happen and I don't know what it is."

Tony uneasily looked at me and asked, "Is something going to happen to our family?"

I quickly tuned in to my spirit team, and replied, "No, but it will have a negative impact!"

The feeling got more intense as the week went on, a feeling of 'dread'. I was frustrated that I didn't know why I had this feeling. Then September 11 happened and with that the feeling went away. September 11 was life changing, and devastating for so many.

Another time I remember telling our son John that he was not to go to the school fete when he was a teenager. "Why not?" he questioned. "It's not fair! You're letting Chloe go, why can't I go?"

"I have a bad feeling about it," I replied. It really wasn't fair that I was not letting him go, but I needed to trust my intuition. After a lot of negotiating, it was decided that he could go to a mate's place, but not to the fete. I was taking my mother to the movies and suggested he join us, but that was not a 'cool' thing to do.

When I came out of the movies and turned on my phone, there was a message to go to the hospital, as John was injured. His mate and his family had all decided to attend the fete, so he went with them. John didn't want to tell them that for no reason that he knew of, he was forbidden from going there. I immediately went to the hospital and discovered that John had fractured a growth plate in his foot on a blow-up slide, when someone bigger and lot heavier landed on him. I now knew the exact reason why I didn't want him to go to the fete.

We have come to the end of this book and by all means I don't profess that you are going to have found all your answers in the previous pages. Like you, I am learning and discovering even more secrets, of 'how to become more psychic'.

It seems like it was not so long ago I was learning the basics and wanting to know how to work with my seemingly out-of-control powers. I, too, have walked the same path that many of you are on to get to where I am now. To this date, I have read for many, created two oracle decks, won awards, written articles for magazines, have appeared on psychic TV and have even been fortunate enough to be on the cover of an international psychic magazine. I love my 'job' and I am proud to have had the opportunity to assist in the development of many psychics, and to help numerous people through providing readings and guidance.

I like to teach through 'stories', to provide relatable examples, and most importantly, where possible, proof. I will continue to question and look for proof, and I encourage you to do the same. At this stage, I no longer teach to one-on-one clients, as it is more economical to buy my online courses, that you can do at your own pace, wherever or whenever you desire.

My dearest wish is that many of you will start to recognise the signs that let you know that you are on the right path. Learn to believe in you and trust in your abilities. Yes, you can do this! Follow your intuition and practise to strengthen that muscle. The glorious thing about your spiritual path is that there is no end; it can be ongoing for as long as you wish to follow it. We don't need to know what the end of our journey is going to be, we just need to be open, to learn

Life as a Psychic

and trust. For some of you this could be the start of your journey and for others, clarification of what could be, or what you can look forward to.

Think of this book as just the beginning rather than the end of your path to becoming more psychic, and I hope you enjoy every step you take along this amazing passage in your life.

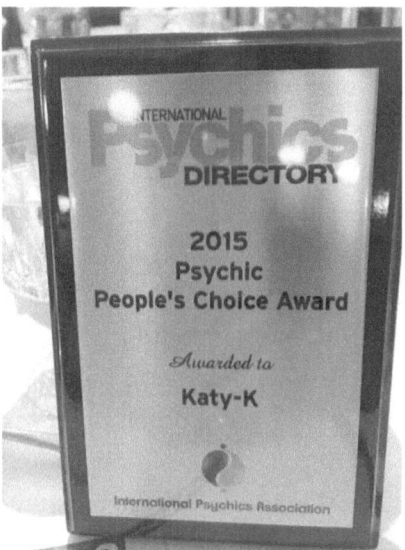

Testimonials

What People Are Saying About Katy-K

I would like to praise and thank Katy for the wonderful, accurate and inspiring reading I had the privilege to have with her; she stunned me with her accuracy about myself as a person and about my twin daughters. She also gave me an insight about developing my spirituality and inspired me to consider developing my inner psychic intuition; I am so looking forward to meeting Katy in England later in the year. Thank you so much again.

Barbara

The Modern Oracle

Usually people scale rate their readings between 1 and 10 but Katy is a singularity and in a class of her own. Katy possesses a variable intuitive aptitude of ability and it's crystal clear that Katy is on top of her game. Katy's reading exceeded my every expectation and the range of her flawless accuracy kept me energised and engaged throughout the entire reading. Katy revealed blockages and issues that were hindering my life, past and present, and identified the processes I needed to instil in order to move forward into the future. Katy also scanned my chakra column and cleared the energy meridians and made me feel awesome instantly. Katy adorned my reading with an immeasurable spiritual dynamic that is unsurpassed and world class. I highly recommend Katy to anyone seeking happiness and fulfilment in their lives and wish Katy every success life has to offer.

Shafiq

I just wanted to write a truly well-deserved testimonial for Katy. I have never had a reading done by anyone before. Katy has left me speechless at everything she knew about me when I hadn't even told her anything. She gained my trust and I knew I could trust everything she was telling me. Katy is straight to the point but she is warm. She made me feel relieved and at ease, she answered all my questions and covered every emotion I was feeling. She knew about my family and certain situations and I feel so blessed that Katy has been able to help me. I felt like I was on the phone to my best friend. Katy is a beautiful woman with a wonderful gift and I'm so glad I got the chance to speak to her.

Sue-Ellen

Wow! I really enjoyed your workshop. Fantastic, informative and so much fun. I learnt so much and now feel confident to go out and put it all into practice. Can't wait for your next workshop.

Sandra

Testimonials

Katy was able to connect with not only myself, but my grandmother who passed away before I was born. I found the reading to be amazingly accurate down to tiny details which came as a surprise to me that Katy could even have known of them. The reading has helped me to look at various aspects of my life and to trust my intuition. I would not hesitate to recommend Katy and would love to have another reading from her in the future. Thank you!

Kathryn

Katy has been reading my cards for at least four years and in that time has provided readings that are inspirational and revelational. Katy told me that I would buy a property near the water and within two years, this was the case. She also told me that I would need to consider my health and take that side of my life extremely seriously. Within a year I found out that I had breast cancer. She also told me not to worry about the cancer, that I would overcome the situation; within one year I have beaten the cancer and am in remission. My experience with each reading has been extremely thought-provoking and I find Katy to be an inspirational teacher and a sincere guide who is a support to all.

Julianne

I just feel like I need to write another testimonial for Katy because I have just had a second reading done and all I can say is WOW!!! Honestly, Katy is beautiful in every way possible. I trust her with all my heart and absolutely recommend Katy to everyone. Katy is so helpful and helped put my mind at ease; she has helped me let go of what is not worth holding on to and allowed me to just be happy and live my life.

Sue

The Modern Oracle

This was my first-ever experience with any sort of psychic reading and I have to say it was such a delightful and informative experience. Katy was incredibly warm and personable and made me feel so comfortable. The information that she had insight to was amazing and she really led me to find the clarity and confirmation that I was after. I will definitely recommend Katy to friends and family! Many thanks!

Callie

Katy-K is a wonderful mentor and teacher. Teaching in a very clear, precise way.

Julie

Enlightening and thorough. Always interesting information. Katy's teaching style has always made learning easy. I always come away feeling positive and encouraged to improve and develop.

Regina

Katy has given me full confidence and courage to open up and come out of my shell and to accept my spiritual ability.

Colleen

Fabulous class that makes a complex subject simple, straightforward, practical and fun.

Andrea

Katy-K allowed me to realise my potential with life. It is an exciting thought, to think and believe anything is possible.

Amanda

Testimonials

Katy is an accomplished psychic medium and healer. Her delivery is considered, articulate and most importantly, grounded. I am always appreciative of her time.

Paul

It is so comforting to know that there are people like Katy in the world. To feel such a connection and hear words that are so close to our hearts.

Shayne

Katy's reading was fantastic, very insightful and spot on. Gave me very important information to continue my spiritual journey.

Deb

Katy-K knew everything that was going on—past, present and future—without me saying anything!

Skye-Louise

What People Are Saying About *The Modern Oracle* Deck

A very easy-to-use deck, so many levels to each card; even if you pulled the same cards for two people (highly unlikely) the meanings would be different. Have never met a deck like it. It's my go-to.
Mandi Louise—Rated 5 out of 5

The only deck I use in my spiritual practice is *The Modern Oracle* deck. The words and picture combination is easy to use. I get so many intuitive hits when I use the cards. A simple one-card reading gives me so much information. When I do readings for other people, they come back to me with amazing validations and confirmations. A beginner can use *The Modern Oracle* cards right out of the box. All Katy's online courses are extraordinary and she goes above and beyond to offer support to the student community. 10/10 would recommend.

Valerie—Rated 5 out of 5

I'd like to share my satisfaction with *The Modern Oracle* deck with you. I absolutely love them!!! Like most people I was bit sceptical in the beginning as I was using other decks, but I decided to give them a go and get them. I'm so glad I did because they are sooooo easy to use, they are very accurate and I love the whole design of them with the pictures. Great job, Katy! Since I purchased them, I have not been using anything else, truly! For those who are still hesitating I'd definitely recommend them.

Petra—Rated 5 out of 5

Your *Modern Oracle* cards are amazing; I've done several readings in the past week and they are absolutely spot on. I love the way they tell the story, no need to use another deck for clarification or confirmation. You are just so clever!

Tracee—Rated 5 out of 5

I love the new *Modern Oracle* deck! The cards are the perfect size for shuffling, the images are beautiful and the words written on the images make it so easy for you to interpret the messages. You can use the deck to form sentences, use as a 'timeline' of past/present/future or just to guide you or the person you are reading for. This deck is so straightforward and so simple to use, it is easy for beginners and also for experienced readers. I totally recommend this deck, I love it!

Sue—Rated 5 out of 5

What People Are Saying About
The Modern Oracle of Essential Oils Deck

From the moment I opened this box I knew I was holding something special! These cards are unique, and something I have never seen before. You can use them for a daily affirmation, chakra colour, essential oil or herb to add to your daily ritual. The messages given on each card are easy to read and understand. This is a great tool to use with clients, or to treat yourself to a daily message and affirmation for the day. I also found the cards blended well when using with the original *Modern Oracle* deck. Thank you, Katy-K, for making such a beautiful deck of oracle cards. My new favourite deck of cards!

Kati—Rated 5 out of 5

The Modern Oracle

I received these cards just last week and already I am in love with them. I have always been interested in aromatherapy and I do use essentials oils in any of my healings with clients, so to now have this deck as part of my toolkit is wonderful as I can use them to tell clients which essential oils they may need to work with to heal their chakras. This card deck is gentle and very colourful and warm. I already feel comfortable in using them, after only one week of them arriving.

Merendi—Rated 5 out of 5

I love these cards; I draw a card every day, and after hearing Katy-K talk about the cards and the meanings I feel connected to them even more.

Kate Strong—Rated 5 out of 5

Love this deck and use them for daily guidance and to select oils to support health and wellbeing. 100% accuracy, excellent information on the oils, messages are intuitive and affirmations will change your thought patterns; each card is colour coded according to the chakras and numerology is also in play with the cards. Beautifully presented and you get to see the source of each oil. Don't hesitate, such a beautiful tool and deck of guidance for everyday use.

Jules Impiccini—Rated 5 out of 5

This deck is amazing with seven ways to use it. I use both Katy-K's decks as they are both so accurate it is mind blowing. This deck comes with both messages and affirmations. You can use them to check chakras and they are numbered for numerology as well as using it in conjunction with Katy's first deck. I no longer use any other decks. Well done, Katy-K.

Stephanie M—Rated 5 out of 5

Testimonials

Congratulations, Katy-K, on your marvellous achievement to be judged *Runner-Up* for *Aspiring Debut Author* in the International Tarot Foundation prestigious Carta Awards 2020. This award is well deserved with so many voting for *The Modern Oracle of Essential Oils* deck. Well done, Katy-K, you had my vote!

V. Mason

Offers

- 20% off Psychic Development 101 at www.katy-k.thinkific.com with the discount code 'KTKBOOK20'

- A free meditation at www.katy-k.thinkific.com

- Free mini course at www.katy-k.thinkific.com

Contact Details for Katy-K

Email: ktkacademy@gmail.com

Website: www.katy-k.com

Online courses and meditations: www.katy-k.thinkific.com

About the Author

Australian-born Katy-K is a spiritual junkie who loves travelling the world always looking for her next 'energy' hit.

With a family background of psychic mediums Katy has spent more than thirty years passionately developing her gifts. She has studied with some of the best in the business worldwide and continues to pass on that knowledge and produce many professional psychics.

The Modern Oracle

When Katy is not pursuing her passion, she is driving her loving husband crazy with all the 'side effects' of being psychic. Her other passions are family, dogs, reading, Zumba and saving the koalas.

Award-winning Katy-K is the creator of *The Modern Oracle* and *The Modern Oracle of Essential Oils* decks.

Katy was recently awarded 'Runner-Up' for the prestigious Carta Awards 2020 for 'Aspiring Debut Author' by the International Tarot Foundation, which has entries from Tarot and Oracle creators worldwide.

To learn more about Katy-K visit her website *www.katy-k.com*

Speakers Bio

'Katy-K' is an international psychic medium, tutor and known as the Modern Oracle.

Having created two very popular oracle decks, *The Modern Oracle* and *The Modern Oracle of Essential Oils,* she then went on to write her first book *The Modern Oracle – How to Tap Into Your Unique Psychic Powers*. Katy also holds the privilege of being awarded the International Psychics Directory '2015 Psychic People's Choice Award'.

With more than thirty years of experience Katy loves passing on her knowledge and has tutored many students who have gone on to become professional psychic readers and tutors. Katy's approach to teaching is that it should be easy and fun, and she likes to take the stress out of learning. It is her mission to teach simpler ways to develop your intuitive gifts and has modernised the way it is taught with many online courses and meditations.

The Modern Oracle

An in-demand and engaging speaker, Katy has been a guest presenter at Mind Body Spirit Festivals, psychic expos, podcasts and Psychic TV. She also regularly demonstrates her abilities on social media.

Katy currently speaks and runs workshops on the following topics and each topic can be customised to your specific audience:

- Becoming more psychic
- Getting started on your psychic journey
- Seven steps to becoming more psychic
- Five steps to spiritual connection
- Mastering *The Modern Oracle*
- Setting up to do a psychic reading
- Readings with *The Modern Oracle* decks

To enquire about engaging Katy-K to speak at your next event, please email for pricing and availabilities.

Notes

The Modern Oracle

Notes

The Modern Oracle

Notes

www.ingramcontent.com/pod-product-compliance
Lightning Source LLC
Chambersburg PA
CBHW021436080526
44588CB00009B/557